Happily Ever After In The Real World

The Roadmap for a Fulfilling Relationship

Nothing Beats Experience!

Happily Ever After In The Real World

The Roadmap for a Fulfilling Relationship

Nothing Beats Experience!

Anne Benissan

ISBN-13: 978-0-9911615-0-8

DEDICATION

To my friends who inspired me to investigate
what works in helping relationship last,
and to all the couples who are willing
to nurture their relationship.

CONTENTS

TO MY DEAR HUSBAND

If it were not for my life with you
I would not have written this book.
Our relationship is my primary reference
in order to help other couples thrive the way we do.

Words cannot describe my love and respect for you.
Thank you so much for your ongoing support
in each of my endeavors.

TO MY WONDERFUL CHILDREN

I would also like to thank each of you for all the questioning
and the discernment you have triggered while growing.
Thank you so much for your love, trust and patience.

With all my love,
Anne

NOTE TO YOU DEAR READER

This book is initially an e-Book and all the references are web links. Some URLs were quite long so I shortened all the links and placed them in footnotes for your easy access.

INTRODUCTION

This book champions long-term relationships, faithfulness, and the value of a commitment. It provides the tools and insights that will give you the key to unlock your own relationship so that it enriches you and brings you joy and fulfillment.

Unlike most books on relationships, this one talks about what can affect them in the light of modern life. You might be surprised to see that a lot of critical factors are outside of the relationship. If you try to improve a relationship by only focusing on the couple's interactions, regardless of external factors such as individual's well being, work life balance, and the presence of children, you are bound to fail in the long run. Couples who want to last should assess the situation from a broader perspective than the relationship itself, and find exactly what needs to change. The key to improve a relationship might then well be outside the relationship. Our western world is changing before our eyes on many levels: technology deeply reforms our lives. We must adapt to new ways of communicating, making money, getting a job, and much more. Our beliefs are mostly based on what was known regardless of whether or not the reasoning behind the belief is still valid. Until a new idea creates new beliefs we must stay curious in order to be able to seize the opportunities for a better life that lay before us.

Love and respect should be at the base of any relationship, and no one should stay in an abusive relationship. I write at length about why I think divorces are detrimental in general. I know however, that in certain circumstances, divorce is the only path.

Men and women have equal rights, even if they have different needs. These differences are precisely what makes the relationship between a man and a woman valuable.

The world we live in presents many new challenges, and if we want relationships to last, we need to reassess all the ideas about gender roles in a relationship that we have inherited. If religious and social pressures are now less likely to prevent separations, what will make couples last?

This leads to another question: is it right to fight against the trend of switching partners and building multiple families along the way?

One could think that this is some kind of new norm that corresponds to modern life, that we should adjust to it instead of fighting against it. Yet, trends are not necessarily good, and while they very often reveal the easy path, it is not necessarily the right one.

A stable relationship fosters social stability and personal growth. The benefits extend to the community level: please take a look at the bulletin on youth residential placement from the <u>Office of Juvenile Justice and Delinquency Prevention</u> (OJJDP)[1], dated December 2010, to find more information on the links between family background and delinquency. When parents are a stable couple, it tends to limit criminality by providing a safe environment for children to grow and become responsible adults. A stable relationship promotes true happiness for everybody because it gives a sense of security to everyone in contact with the couple; it is a small scale version of a democracy. If we succeed in a lasting relationship with someone from the opposite gender when separation is possible, we set a very good foundation at a community level to understand and compromise with those who have a different background or a different way of life than we do.

A relationship is not stable simply because we decide it should be. Vows alone are not enough, and religious boundaries no longer stand in the way, as they once did in many communities.

Besides the desire to make it work, a relationship takes time, energy, and personal introspection. Furthermore, a long-term relationship provides the best opportunities to become a better person.

Being confronted with that which is different silences the ego, and helps us overcome our fears.

After explaining why paying more attention to your relationship is worth your time, I describe a very pragmatic and effective approach to deepen mutual love and respect.

You may be surprised to see chapters about health, parenting, and other subjects that may not seem directly connected to the dynamic of a relationship.

Focusing on relationships without taking into account what deeply

---

[1] http://www.ezcouple.com/ofjjp

influences a couple is as ineffective as ignoring the interconnection of all the organs in the human body when a problem arises in any one of them.

EZcouple.com[2], the site that will replace peacereminder.com soon, is based on this holistic approach, like a turnkey program you can start immediately. I created both sites to help long-term couples nurture their relationship. EZcouple will simply be a better version incorporating the lessons learned from peacereminder.com.

Voltaire, the eighteenth-century French philosopher said, "Le mieux est l'ennemi du bien," which translates as "The best is the enemy of the good."

EZcouple works for the good, not for the best. It is not meant to replace counseling, or restore constructive communication by itself, but it can greatly increase our efficiency in showing our love and care for our partner in our busy lives, when free time is scarce. Just as we now need to schedule exercise to make sure we move enough in our otherwise sedentary lifestyle, we also must be proactive in nurturing our relationship on a conscious level.

Relationships are everything but an exact science with automatic answers. This is what makes them so fascinating. I share with you my humble understanding from my global perspective and my own experience.

My childhood and early adult life have led me to take a close look at major psychology theories, including most psychotherapy and emotional release techniques. My interest in helping couples has led me to read as much as I could on relationship-improvement techniques and theories. They all have merits but they tend to focus on one side of the problem, therefore presenting a biased view of the challenges couples face today.

Along the way I mention all the techniques that I found valuable with the references so that you can find and use them if you want to.

I hope my book gives you a clear understanding of what you should focus on to improve your own relationship.

This is meant to help. I hope it will!

---

[2] http://www.ezcouple.com

"Women marry men hoping they will change.
Men marry women hoping they will not.
So each is inevitably disappointed."

Albert Einstein

1

PITFALLS IN LONG-TERM RELATIONSHIPS

A loving relationship is by far one of the most exciting and fulfilling of human experiences. The relationship instills in us a state of well-being that ranges from happiness to unprecedented bliss.

What happens between two individuals in a loving relationship has been written, painted, and sung about since the beginning of human time. However, these enchanting descriptions can mislead us by suggesting what the nature of a relationship should be in the long run. The level of excitement praised by poets, writers, singers, and authors of all kinds, is in most cases, only sustainable for a relatively short period of time. For centuries in what we know as the western world today, relationships were so tied to marriage and religious celebrations that the social focus was not on the relationship after marriage. Focus in the past, was mainly on the stage that precedes procreation, in order to ensure the survival of the human species. Marriages were binding contracts and could not be terminated. Times have changed, life is longer, and marriage has lost the lifetime binding commitment it used to imply. Yet, belief systems regarding relationships have not really changed, and we are faced today with an unprecedented lack of commitment in relationships: not only heterosexual marriages have been in decline for the past thirty years, but relationships, within a marriage or not, seem to have a real difficulty to last. You can check the numbers in Part 2: (marriage crisis) of this chapter. The result of this imbalance is that some of the fundamentals of our society are threatened: the primary trust and faith in the other are challenged by the precariousness of family ties. Repercussions and consequences are particularly important in children because it deprives them from the candid time when emotional stability is key, molding their adult relationships along the way.

It is therefore time to take a closer look at the bundle of emotions that motivate us, so we can reconcile our individual needs and a long lasting relationship.

Part 1: Long-Term Relationship Dangers

Misconception About What To Expect

We could blame the trend of individualism for challenging long-term relationships. And it probably plays a big role in the contemporary problems relationships face.

I think however that there is a deeper root: the outdated conception of what a couple is and should be. Expectations for both men and women have become distorted, leading to misconception about what the other gender wants and needs, and disappointment.

Women are bathed in Barbie pink almost from birth, raised with Disney fairy tales' myth that a woman's happiness depends on a man's rescue and love. Consciously, or more likely unconsciously, our ideal partner is an imaginary Prince Charming. Some men can be Prince Charming in the seductive stage of a relationship, but often the charm is used to get what they want. Once they have spent some time in the relationship, the charm may disappear. Men, on the other hand, are raised with the different but equally misleading image of their mother: a woman is the one who will look after him with gentleness, concern, and unconditional love. Their assumption is that a man's wife will be as patient and loving as Mommy, with sex as a bonus. The marital home will be the safe haven the man can go back to whenever needed.

Once in a relationship, however, both partners slowly but surely realize how false these images are. Women soon find that Prince Charming has become Mr. Selfish, and men soon find that the gentle princess has become Mrs. Nagging, or Mrs. Unsatisfied, or Mrs. Demanding, or each of them in turn!

So have the two partners intrinsically changed in the course of the relationship? No and yes.

No, they have not changed, because all our perceptions are biased when we are in the "honeymoon" phase of a relationship. This is the period when the other partner is just perfect. This is the period when all that matters is to show the best of ourselves to convince our partner that we are his or her perfect partner as well. We are deeply motivated. This is human, and this is fair. Seduction is the best motivation of all in terms of mobilizing your energy. Once we have "secured" a partner, our goal is achieved. For men in particular, the hunter within is satisfied, and a new hunt starts: a prestigious job to provide for his family, social achievement, and so on. For women, a shift occurs too, usually when she has conceived a child. Therefore the attention both men and women pay to each other gradually drifts away. This is the first reason they have changed. In addition, from birth to death, life is nothing but a cycle of transformations. We are constantly changing, evolving, reforming, and transforming. Is transformation the problem? Certainly not, or we would have a hundred percent divorce rate. Transformation, though, means adjustments. And you need to be willing to overcome the problems, to make it work. The key to success in a relationship is acceptance of your own weaknesses and the knowledge that you can change. Acceptance is not resignation. If you accept your own not-so-perfect side, then it is much easier to accept your partner with his or her own weaknesses. You can then become proactive partners in your relationship, beyond that initial stage of passion.

This acceptance is what love is truly about. Passion deserves a closer look because the energy it carries is such a fuel.

Passion is magic. It sweeps us away, and we all thrive on this type of energy. It feels wonderful because things seem to happen effortlessly, and our view of the world is filtered through our happiness, keeping negativity at bay. There is a lot to learn from this amazing time when you have found your mate. You are still discovering each other, and excitement rules your life. Just thinking about that time lifts you up: the usual lack of energy or boredom is gone. But what is passion, exactly? As a feeling, it may not be easy to describe. Passion has three characteristic components:

- Novelty
- Chemistry
- Desire

Although the third factor is by far the most important one, let's start with the concept of **Novelty**. Some cultures favor novelty more than others. In Asia, for instance, from what I have seen in Singapore, Bangkok, and Hong Kong, there is a cultural attraction to novelty and change. What is new must be tried. In France, on the other hand, novelty triggers suspicion. And unless the new idea gets enough social approval, what is new is, in general, initially rejected.

When it comes to our relationships, though, we all long for something new that makes us feel good. Our natural curiosity thrives on the unknown. The discovery process triggered by a new relationship is a fascinating and irresistible road. Not all that is new is created equally valuable, however. We must have enough information about the new in order to understand it, and for it to be pleasant to us. If it is totally unknown, it becomes frightening. The beginning of a relationship is amazingly stimulating because it sustains the excitement without ever being frightening. The partner has this novelty that challenges our imagination. What is new, then, becomes a potential opportunity, and women are far savvier when diving into potential than men. What most men do not realize during the "honeymoon" phase is that most women are already four steps ahead of them. Very early in the relationship, she is already imagining what kind of husband and father her partner could be. What he imagines is totally different: he pictures his partner's ongoing burning desire for him. He dreams about her passion and enthusiasm for him lasting forever. The good or bad news, depending on how we see it, is that neither of them shares his or her dreams with the other yet. This passionate state is too good to be spoiled by reality. It is new; we have plenty of time!

Chemistry is a major factor sustaining this passionate state. Our body's biochemistry fuels the desire. All kinds of sensors are on alert, and all senses are responsive. Hormonal systems on both sides work full speed creating an addictive desire for the other. The mind is fully in agreement with this physical desire: everything about the new relationship is designed to trigger these good feelings. This is why we unconsciously build memories about places to which we have been, songs to which we have listened, fragrances smelled, and skin sensations felt. These triggers are embedded subconsciously so that as soon as any of the five senses are stimulated the same way, the emotional part of the brain experiences the same positive feelings. As a result, biochemistry fuels romance for months and sometimes years. Subconscious recollection triggers that chemistry.

None of the above would kick in, though, if there were not a burning **Desire** at the source. This is one confirmation that the subconscious part of the mind drives everything else. If it were not for a specific desire, we would mate with the first person from the opposite sex whose hormonal stage would match ours. The attraction would be purely physical, and would be the ground of a relationship unsustainable in the long run. Successful copulation would be the leading factor. There is no romance in that kind of interaction. The desire I am referring to here is the mental willingness to make the relationship work beyond the sexual intercourse, the mental ability to love. We proactively look for everything we can love in the other person. This desire is in fact a combination of multiple desires, and that is what makes it so powerful. Let's list these multiple desires: the desire to feel good about oneself; the desire to be accepted; the desire to be loveable; the desire to be touched lovingly; the desire of the fusion achieved during sex; the desire to be important; the desire to be needed; the desire to grow and procreate. All these desires make up the core of our identity: our self-confidence depends on their fulfillment. And more importantly, our happiness depends on that fulfillment as well. Having a fulfilling life while single seems therefore unlikely, because the key to unlock access to our potential as a human being is missing. When this desire is transformed into love, we have access to our true self, and we can become a better person. The other is not only a support, but also a mirror, forcing us to go beyond what we would like to see in ourselves.

What is important to remember here is that passion is based on desires that have very little to do with our partner. It is driven by the absolute necessity for us to feel good at some point about ourselves. We are unconsciously looking for the partner that will patch the holes in our love tank. Our love tank is a symbolic gauge revealing our ability to be positively opened to others: love could be seen as a food necessary to thrive. The love tank is the storage for that particular food. When that tank is empty, we are in survival mode and primarily focused on ourselves. What love teaches us, though, is that love wounds are healed first from within, in our heart and mind. Unless you truly love yourself, you can't love anybody else. If we don't love our self, feeling loved becomes increasingly difficult because we are in constant search of a confirmation that we are worthy to be loved, and we become a prey to all sorts of abuse either at the work place or in our personal life. Passion will hide this truth for some time but not for long. It is therefore critical to understand the fact that any loving interaction with someone else is first a loving interaction with oneself. When passion fades, only you can decide to reignite it. The best way to do that is to find something, not someone, about which you can be passionate. Most likely your passion will fulfill you at a deep level too. Your being will expand, and you will be able to experience love at a deeper level, too. This energy will motivate you to express more love, and therefore attract more love. And more importantly, it will guide your life.

Those who look into a passionate replacement relationship in order to feel good are misled by the illusion that long lasting passion will come from outside of them.

True passion comes from within. It is fueled by the things we do, and the thoughts we have, that make us feel good. Usually passion is meant to be, and creates excellence. Talent is nothing more than acknowledged passion.

True love between two people starts when they are each able to see, respect and foster the other's passion for something else than their relationship.

Too often we perceive our partner's passion with skepticism or defiance. This only reflects our own insecurity and lack of self-confidence. There is no reason to feel threatened by our loved one's passion if we have our own. On the contrary, our support is essential to our partner's success because we are the only one close enough to motivate our loved one when doubts arise, or when comfort is needed. Our encouragement is priceless.

We all want to believe that passion will never fade in the relationship. At the beginning, we know all the pitfalls we have observed in others, and we all think that, for us, it will be different. Then life intrudes, routine steps in, and slowly but surely we are all so absorbed by daily life that soon our partner isn't receiving much attention from us. This may be sad, but it is normal. Priorities have changed. There are so many things that are so important aside from the relationship! In addition, both men and women wrongly think that they are doing their part because they both base their actions on what they believe they should do instead of closely investigating what needs to be done. The remembrance of the initial life commitment is perceived as a safety net they can trust. As time passes, however, miscommunication and frustration build up if nothing is done proactively to nurture the relationship.

Nurturing the relationship without devoting all your energy to it is not an easy task. And this is especially true for men. This is why I am building EZcouple.com, a tool for the busy couple who cares about their relationship. EZcouple, improved version of PeaceReminder.com, can help men achieve success with their own wife almost effortlessly, while making their wife feel really special.

Miscommunication And Nagging

Nagging is a recurrent complaint men have about their relationship. Almost every website giving advices on marriages have a dedicated section to the nagging. It is known as a silent killer for a passionate relationship. I could not find official data on that matter, but there are articles describing the problem, you can read <u>this one written by Elisabeth Bernstein from the Wall Street Journal, published on January 12th 2012</u>[3]. Men can nag as well, but it seems that women are more prone to nag. Most of the time women start nagging about household tasks. Then it gradually becomes the way for the wife to communicate most requests. Women and men do not focus on the same things when it comes to their household. What matters for one partner may be irrelevant to the other. Tidiness and cleanliness are critical for her, rarely for him. Home for him is the space where he unwinds, and relaxes his vigilance. So, he genuinely does not see that the garbage must be taken out. The weekly schedule of garbage disposal is not even on his radar. Yet for her, it is frustrating and annoying, and it shows.

We are all trained to distribute and share domestic tasks, but nobody truly gives instructions on how to do that. We should view allocating

---

3 http://www.ezcouple.com/WSJ011212

these tasks through the perspective of speaking different languages. When we are in a different country, we try our best to speak in order to be understood. Female partners should do this in their relationship.

Often women feel entitled to some help without defining precisely what help they need. What needs to be done is so obvious to them that they presume that any sane person would notice too. They forget that men are different: men will not pay attention to what they view as details.

It takes a rational, goal-oriented approach to get the man's radar up, running, and aware.

Women should convey their message so that it is received and understood by the recipient. Nagging does not work in the long run. As time goes, more nagging will be necessary to any results, and the man has not fully bought into whatever the task is. He is performing the task purely out of exasperation, to make the nagging stop. The more she nags, the less he listens to her. Miscommunication gradually worsens. Yet, men are willing to help if we bother explaining to them precisely what we need.

We should take the time to sit down together, review all the domestic duties we have on our plates, and identify the ones we can share. Both partners should be truly honest about how they feel about each task. You might be surprised to find out that what is cumbersome for you may not be for your partner. Once a task has been assigned, detail what you each expect as a result, but let the assignee decide the way the task is going to be handled. The art of delegating lies in not being a control freak. Whatever is decided is not carved in stone either. In fact, both partners should review the task delegation regularly to make sure it makes a positive change in their lives.

Men would much rather help than be nagged. Nagging is a kind of torture that they would like to avoid at any cost.

For those of you ladies who feel that delegating tasks is more complicated than anything else, even when you are eager to get his help, if you stick to the recommendations above you will soon notice two different results:

1. Very often you are better off doing what you want yourself.

2. What was a burden for you is nothing for him, and you will regret the time you spent on that task before letting it go.

When perspectives and priorities differ, it takes constant, clear communication to make things work. Naggers will claim that they are communicating their desires. Unfortunately, desires that come in the shape of nagging are a blurry message for men. Bear in mind that men have no interest in what they are nagged about; otherwise there would be no nagging. If their attention is not carefully drawn, they will not get the message. On the matter of nagging in particular, I believe that women who work outside their home nag far less than those who don't. First, they don't have time to nag, and second, their focus is elsewhere, so they let go much more when it comes to domestic tasks. Women who work in the business world are by necessity also far better communicators with men. They do that all day in the workplace! They most likely will express their desires in a way that will be understandable for any man, including their partner. Even so, they still may forget to use one technique that has proven to be amazingly efficient in my household. Whenever I have something in mind that I would love my husband to do, I send him a brief email. I use the subject line for the task, and I try to be concise and precise in the content of the email. Bullet points are great to shorten sentences. Invariably, I get an email back within the hour: "Got it. Will do". And he does. The beauty of email for communicating about "boring" tasks that are important to women should be highlighted. What happens in the male mind is this: he understands the email as important because his brain is patterned to get significant tasks via email. Additionally, there is no tone of voice that could carry some negative emotional charge. So the brain gladly adds it to the to-do list, and triggers the usual reminders men use to stay on track. Furthermore, a man who comes home after work is not particularly inclined to talk. So something that is boring to him will not easily catch his attention as a topic of conversation. We could debate endlessly why men should not find the details that matter to women boring. The point is that nagging reflects something important for her that he should take care of, in order for him not to be nagged. Nagging will stop when both genders stop presuming that the other one knows, without discussion, what needs to be done. Our perspectives are different from our partner's, and that shows every day if we pay attention. The good news is that this is why as couples, we can't argue forever: we don't pay attention to the same things. Take a look at women's arguments with each other. It's a completely different story from a mixed gender argument's perspective. No wonder the recurring arguments between mother and daughter are so difficult for men to understand! Often the source of a female conflict is quite meaningless for men: men would not feel offended for the same things. Men and women's perspectives are complementary. This book aims to teach you how to make use of them so that both partners benefit from these differences.

A few guidelines to keep nagging at bay:

1. Whenever possible, ladies, actually take action for what truly matters to you. If you need help, take the steps to find it. Don't wait for your partner's approval.

2. Explain what you want in writing, via an email, with as much detail as possible, and explain how important it is to you. Send that email in a timely manner, not too early, not too late. Timely means that the time you choose to send it is rather defined by the necessary

average preparation needed to perform a task, than by your own anxiety around the fact that it might not be done.

3. Gentlemen, explain why you are not doing something that your wife has asked you to do, if it is something more than "I forgot." If you did just forget, add a reminder on your calendar.

4. Discuss the issue before it heats up. You may find that you need to split the tasks or trade them for something else, like fixing dinner for cleaning up. Don't try to understand why your priorities differ, just accept that they do, and act upon that.

Both nagging and the increasing frustration that results will miraculously stop.

When passion wanes, and misunderstandings build up, the easy road might be to look for the same thrill in another partnership elsewhere. The relationship you are "stuck with" may seem to require so much maintenance that the temptation of another relationship may appear to be the relief of not having to work so hard. That NEW person seems to be so much more fun, understanding, and loving! But how real is that?

The Exciting Appeal Of Affairs

Infidelity is always a bad idea. The transgression of affairs goes far beyond the limits of social conventions backed by religion. Furthermore all affairs lead astray.

Passion is temporary. The grass is not greener on the other side. The lure of infidelity is always deceptive. The chill you have, the heartbeat, and the energy you suddenly have in an affair may be worth it for a short time, but know that this other magical being is usually just your current partner in disguise.

There are two reasons for that:

1. Whether you like it or not, unless you have worked on your feelings and emotions for some time, you are attracted to the same type of partner with the same flaws. And it won't be long before you realize that. This realization may partially explain why divorce rates increase after the first marriage. Check out this site edivorcepapers. com[4] for more data on divorce rates. Mr. or Ms. New Partner is merely a disguised replica of the former Mr. or Ms. Partner in terms of what you didn't like. It is only a matter of time before passion wanes and you become aware of that similarity with your former partner.

2. You are sinking deep into myriad troubles that will affect everybody, including you. Either you endure the stress of keeping it secret, or your partner happens to find out from you, or worse, from someone else. With life as it is today, how much more stress can you truly handle before collapsing? It will be extremely difficult to heal the wound created by this betrayal. If you have children, they will be in the front row to witness the collapse of your marriage and the emotional traumas that go with it. When adults are hurt, badly hurt, don't expect them to be in control of their behavior. The primary reflex of anyone who has been hurt is to hurt back. Pain eventually diminishes, but while it is felt, it keeps you from seeing your priorities clearly, including the protection of children.

In other words, an affair is the best way to jeopardize your relationship with little hope of recovery.

Why is infidelity so appealing that sites like AshleyMadison, which encourage married women to commit adultery, are really successful?

From a woman's perspective, it is very clear. A woman is tempted only if she feels a deep vacuum in her relationship. In other words, she does not feel loved, she feels neglected. A husband who travels a lot,

---

4 http://www.ezcouple.com/edivorce

for example, may be unaware that each trip increases the neglect felt by his wife. He may be traveling that much to make sure he provides for her. Nevertheless, she will feel neglected if he does not do the small things she needs him to do in order to feel loved. A romantic affair can make her feel worthy again. She will be special to someone again. She is then misled into this sexual relationship, so she can feel alive and worthy again. What she does not realize is that a man who is not there to give love manipulates her. That man quickly learns to make the right promises to keep the affair going until he is tired of it. Promises, especially the ones that are not honored, don't cost much to the one who makes them.

I suspect that, from a male perspective, the appeal for an affair is nothing more than another need that has become a craving. A faithful man can be tempted to cheat if there has been no sex in his relationship for a long time. Whether we like it or not, most men need to have sex; it is biological. Of course, as they grow older, the need is not as urgent, but it continues to play a significant role in their virility and self-image. They are also tempted by the fact that, once again, they will feel like the Ultimate Guy. This is when his wife's attitude makes him feel wonderful: what she says, or what she does triggers an intense sense of satisfaction.

If women knew how empowering it is for men to feel like the Ultimate Guy, they would not neglect men's needs for a simple communication, and for relaxation the way they do shortly after the passion of a relationship is gone. Similarly, if men realized how important and critical it is for their wife to feel special, they would not begin to take for granted what she does for him soon after a few years of sharing their daily lives.

What both genders forget when they slide into infidelity is that a cheater is a cheater. What this cheating partner has done with you, he or she can easily do again with someone else, at your expense. This is one of the reasons trust is so difficult to restore in a relationship once there's been a betrayal. Your partner might have been making mistakes with you for years. He or she may not understand what you mean when you think you're being clear, but this partner has been sharing your life for a period long enough for you to truly be yourself. You may not like everything about you when you are with your partner; we all have parts of ourselves that we would rather change. This change however has little to do with your partner; I will develop that idea in the next chapter. This partner has always been there, maybe not the way you wanted, but she or he has been with you, next to you, sharing good and bad moments alike with you. At one time, you decided that he or she was the one for you. Life events do change us, but the foundation of what made you choose him or her remains.

Restoring efficient communication with your partner and trying to address what would make you want to look for another partner should be your priority. If you speak the right language, he or she will be willing to change for you, because your speech will come from a place of love, true love. In return, you will receive love.

This communication is the real solution to the void you may feel in your relationship.

If you can't do that, be brave, and just leave. Don't cheat. Not only will you hurt somebody, but you will also deceive yourself. In that case divorce might be a better option. However, divorce should really be viewed as a solution of last resort.

Despite the fact that divorce hurts so many people, it is a common ending to a lot of relationships.

Part 2: Lack Of Commitment: A Marriage In Crisis And Divorce

∽

My Experience With Divorce

The fact of the matter is that long-term relationships in the western world are in bad shape. Before we look at the numbers, let me share with you my own story. It will give you my perspective on divorce from my experiences as a child of divorce, as a lawyer, and as an adult. My experience underscores the thesis of this book, that long-term relationships should be nurtured.

Couples should think twice before they start a nasty divorce. It is a downward spiral with its own momentum, one that is then fueled by the parties' lawyers trying to get the best possible deal for their respective clients.

I have rarely seen a "good" divorce where the partners end their official relationship respectfully, with no negative repercussions.

For those of you who still believe that it is better to divorce than to have your kids witness your continuing arguments, let me tell you that all kids of divorces have an extensive inside view of their parents' conflicts. Parents' mood and availability are directly affected by those conflicts, and children without really understanding the details, feel sadness that they will try their best to hide. Surface-level and underlying conflicts at home are strongly felt by children regardless of their age. A divorce in itself is a frightening situation and deeply unsettling for a child. It is like choosing Charybdis over Scylla: children suffer no matter what.

After describing my experience when my parents divorced I will address what I have come to believe as an adult.

I was fifteen when my parents started the dreadful process of divorce.

The years before, I remember praying that my parents would not divorce when I heard their continual and noisy arguments. I felt horrible when my mother cried, and I always desperately wished I could do something, anything, to stop the unhappiness.

I tried my best to do well at school and ask as little as possible of my parents, hoping that my behavior would mend their fences. As long as my parents lived together, it felt safe, at least in my head. During this difficult period, somehow they managed to make mutually concerted decisions regarding me. Nevertheless, I felt lonely. My sister had been in boarding schools for many years before their divorce proceedings, and she was already an adult when the divorce started. When they separated, however, their common voice about things that concerned me disappeared. I was not totally stupid, and, as a teen, I learned very quickly how to manipulate the situation to my advantage, or rather, to what I thought was my advantage. I suddenly had a freedom that many kids that age could only dream of. I could basically do what I wanted when I wanted, making sure I would choose the parent who would either agree with me or would be too busy to even notice. Nevertheless, I was deeply unhappy. Because I seemed last in my parents' priorities, I felt I had to be totally responsible for myself, even though I was still a kid.

Reflecting back on that time, I am thankful for whatever divine protection I was under during those three years before I moved out. I made many mistakes, but luckily none were too serious. I still felt the need to study well, and that gave me some kind of structure. It could easily have been much worse. During those years, my life had changed radically. My dad had left home, my mom had left home, and the only one left besides me was my dog. In fact, I was sent to live at a friend's house for a year. I would come home to visit my dog, who was being fed by a neighbor. Then the house was sold, and my dog was sent to a foster home. The beloved friend I was staying with saw how devastating each visit to my empty house to see my dog was for me. She tried to support me as much as she could. This friend and her husband were a blessing in my life. The year I spent with them was the most stable one I had throughout the turmoil that preceded and followed the divorce. They were my parents' best friends, and they had succeeded in the difficult task of staying neutral during the divorce. Of course, this neutrality was not the case with others. More than my house, my bedroom, my belongings, my garden, and the sense of family that I never truly got, I missed my dog and the unconditional love she gave me. For years, the last image of my dog before she went to her new home haunted me, and would always bring tears to my eyes.

It took me a long time before I forgave my parents for unconsciously causing that pain.

As my parents focused on money, possessions, and generally hurting each other, each gathering petty testimonies to belittle the other, my concern was my dog. In my teenage mind, my dog was more important than anything else because she was the victim of all of this much more than I thought I was. The sad but accepting look in her eyes the last time I saw her fueled an anger and sadness that took me years to resolve. At that point, my parents were selfish, irresponsible adults who did not deserve my respect. My goal, my obsession, even, was to grow up as fast as possible so I could put distance and space between them and me. There is always an underlying reason, beyond job opportunities, to live abroad. During my parents' divorce, I witnessed the most disgraceful behavior, pettiness, and a grasping hatefulness. I felt devastated seeing two people I loved hurting each other for incomprehensible (to me) reasons.

I need not go into further details about the degrading situations in which my parents unconsciously placed me over those years. I am sure that those situations are very common unfortunately. What I can say is that those experiences shaped my life. And I am so glad I was fifteen and not younger. At least I had some kind of understanding of what was going on. And, most importantly, I was spared the battle over guardianship. Guardianship battles are the worst of the worst. I remember the debate in family law courses over whether kids of a certain age should choose with whom they wanted to live. Although I have a degree in family law, I hate the fact that it deals with subtle worst of humanity in a civilized country. By this, I mean how people behave while divorcing, and how friends of people divorcing behave as well. Between the childishness, hypocrisy and pettiness, we can see the worst of human behavior. I chose the word "subtle" because there is a trend that finds divorce in general normal, as well as the selfishness that is associated with it. Only lawyers, in private, admit what horrendous behaviors they witness. Asking a child to choose which parent to live with is basically asking the child which parent he prefers. As they are growing up, kids' feelings towards their parents often alternate between intense dislike and intense love. It is important for children's developing sense of self, that they feel safe enough to express their anger and resentment, knowing that their parents won't take their negative emotions at face value, and that their parents will still love them. When a child is given the choice of which parent with whom to live, the parent not selected is deeply hurt, though that feeling may be tempered with a sense of relief. The child is aware of the pain his choice caused, and he will be burdened with unnecessary guilt for a long time. Love will be associated with daunting choices. Therefore, the love is never truly satisfying.

As an adult, I can now reflect on that time of my life. All divorces are unique. However, there are some common truths – "red flag" situations, if you will – of which all parents considering divorce should be aware:

1. Most parents, consciously or not, tend to use their children as the ultimate weapon against each other.

2. All kids learn very quickly how to manipulate the situation by leveraging their parents' feelings of guilt and sense of competing with each other.

3. Most parents at some point, are so overwhelmed with fighting with each other that they forget about their children's best interests.

4. It is a miracle when children of divorce don't choose the wrong path, and take excessive risks to gain love and attention.

5. Parents going through divorce forget two facts: they were once in love, and their shared parenthood deserves their mutual respect.

6. Parents overlook the fact that their behavior during and after the divorce will forever shape their relationship with their kids.

7. Parents are unaware of the fact that they will expose themselves to their kids' anger at some point, even if the anger is unfair, and even if it is based on lies that one parent has told about the other. When the children are old enough to really see the divorce as it was, it will be too late to undo the years of anger that have accrued, and the healing process to repair damaged self-esteem and damaged relationships will be that much more difficult.

8. Divorce does nothing to enhance the stature of either parent as a role model. Kids will inherit deeply negative beliefs about relationships that will take a lot of personal work to overcome. The ability to trust and respect others will by no means be spontaneous. It may in fact be a situation where the child develops great difficulty trusting and respecting others who try to get close to him or her.

Never think you are doing your child a favor by divorcing. In the best-case scenario, you are trying to repair your own mistakes. If you feel that your children are safer with your partner kept at a distance, then it reflects poorly on your decision making process in the first place. Why did you choose him or her to father or mother your child? Your initial choice in entering the relationship whether conscious or not can deprive your child from a normal relationship with one parent. When a divorce results in keeping children safe, the parent who wants to protect the children from the other parent is merely repairing his or her own huge mistake. In addition, being a single parent, or the one who lives with the children most, is incredibly difficult as that parent is left with the challenge of providing true guidance.

Many couples marry for the wrong reasons. We might think that, considering the freedom we all have today to marry whom we choose, couples should last longer. Reality proves otherwise.

We all change with circumstances and life events. Before we commit to marriage, most of us think quite seriously about whether or not to take that step.

True love is, among other things, accepting changes in your partner, as long as the partner remains respectful. No relationship is emotionally level: some times are more difficult than others. It takes a great deal of will and action to make a relationship work over time. Ultimately, though, a long-term relationship is a highly rewarding one.

It takes two to fight. Be aware of your own responsibility and participation before blaming your partner for a conflict. A divorce is a sad event. Don't make it pathetic as well.

The analogy that comes to mind when I think about the outcome of divorce is this: divorce is to life what chemotherapy is to your body. Both remove much more than we initially expect them to; both may leave you sick and bald; both can be very long and costly; and neither guarantees the end of your troubles. Life is not a fairytale, but we can choose whether or not we make it a nightmare.

Many of today's parents were children of divorces. One would think they would make a point of making their marriage a success. It seems, however, that their focus is often elsewhere. Some relationships turn out to be so deprived of love and respect that a divorce might be a better option: often though, before the relationship in a marriage reaches this dead zone where love and respect are secondary, so many little actions could have changed the dynamic. Without proper nurturing any relationship is bound to die.

Marriage Crisis

As Kai Ryssdal from National Public Radio's show Marketplace says, "Let's do the numbers!"

Bear in mind that the official data regarding divorce leaves out a growing number of families built outside of marriage. A survey done by the Centers for Disease Control and Prevention between 2006 and 2010 provides many details on cohabitation without marriage. *"The survey of 12,279 women ages 15 through 44 also found that 40 percent of unmarried partners transitioned to marriage within 3 years, according to the Centers for Disease Control and Prevention report. A third of the arrangements stayed intact without marriage, while 27 percent dissolved, the study found,"* says Elizabeth Lopatto in this <u>April 2013 Bloomberg article</u>[5]. You can also view the CDC report on <u>their website</u>[6].

The <u>latest official statistic</u>[7] from the Census Bureau gives a rate of

---

5 http://www.ezcouple.com/blberg040413

6 http://www.ezcouple.com/cdc1

7 http://www.ezcouple.com/censusb

3.4 divorces per 1000 population in the U.S. in 2009, with the states leading in divorce being Nevada (6.7), Arkansas (5.7), Wyoming, and West Virginia (both at 5.2). Note that there is no data for California in that table. The rate for marriages nationwide for the same year is 6.8. In France, l'Institut National d'Etudes Demographiques[8] states that 46.2 percent of all marriages ended in divorce for the year 2011. For the same year, the Office for National Statistics in the United Kingdom[9] estimates the divorce rate at 42 percent.

Why is the divorce rate so high?

Not so far back in the past, before the 1960s, most people did not choose their partner for life. Who one married was decided either by social pressure or one's family. This is still the case in certain countries today: India is one example where families still arrange the marriage of their children, mainly by providing a few potential partners to choose from. This is different from forced marriages performed in certain countries that do not involve the couple's consent at all; these marriages are illegal in the western world.

Many of us, depending on where we come from, are the result of several generations of couples that did not necessarily choose their partner the way we now choose to get married in the western world. Love as a passionate attraction for each other was not the primary focus then. Mainly since the 1970s, at least in western countries, we have had complete freedom to choose our life partners. In most cases, the initial motivation is love. If we feel love, that is, a certainty that this other person is the one, the only one, we believe we will be making a perfect match. However, according to divorcerate.org[10], which provides the latest data and confirms the trends reported above:

Divorce rates all over the world have risen from one to five

8 http://www.ezcouple.com/inedfr
9 http://www.ezcouple.com/ukstats
10 http://www.ezcouple.com/divrate

percentage points between 2000 and 2012.

Countries with the highest divorce rates are Russia, Belarus, Ukraine, Moldova, and the United States. In the U.S., 41 percent of all marriages ended in divorce in 2011. Projections indicate the rate will reach 50 percent in the next decade. In 2011, most divorces occurred when the marriage took place at 20 to 24 years of age.

In 2011, approximately 36.6 percent of women and 38.8 percent of men who married between the ages of 20 to 24 divorced.

Check this article written by <u>Vicki Larson from the Huffington Post dated August 1st 2011</u>[11]: she discusses the assumption that couples without children would be more prone to divorce. As I believe that parenthood is a major stressor for a relationship (please check chapter 4 of this book on that matter) I tend to think that parents with children may be more willing to make it work for the sake of their children. However, among the couples with children who divorce, they may well do so because of children. Children have a unique way of challenging their parents' relationship, one that could lead to misunderstandings, even arguments. I will discuss that later in chapter 4 in this book. For the time being, let's go back to the statistics.

One factor should be taken into account: the marriage rate, in the western world, has been decreasing steadily for the past 20 years. In France and other countries, civil contracts have become an alternative to marriage for documenting an official relationship. While these contracts may make sense for same-sex couples who cannot legally marry, they are a dangerous illusion for heterosexual couples. For many of these couples, the underlying reason for not getting married, now that marriage is a mostly secular institution, is probably a fear of commitment. It seems to be an illusion that separation is easier if you are not married. In fact, dissolving a civil union may be harder for the

---

11 http://www.ezcouple.com/divrate

most vulnerable one in the partnership. This is particularly true for children of civil unions as well. If people knew before they conceived a child what it really takes to be a parent, I am sure birth rates would drop dramatically.

I find this new trend of having children outside of marriage dangerous. That may sound like a Tea Party slogan, but I don't need to be a Republican or driven by any particular religious faith to say that. All it takes is common sense. What people don't seem to understand is that there is no bigger life commitment than having a child with someone. As long as your child lives, your relationship with the other parent of your child will never end. Even if you don't physically see the father or mother of that child, that ex-partner will be like a shadow or a ghost in your life as long as your child lives. Parents who think they can forget about this relationship not only hurt their own child's emotional and psychological wellbeing but also delude themselves. Once you know that having a child is the biggest commitment there is, why not get married to the child's other parent? If you can't face the prospect of growing old with your partner, why on earth would you want a child with that person? Both governments and religious authorities throughout the centuries have significantly encouraged having as many children as possible. Population growth was perceived as a major asset. The only noticeable exception is China who mandated the only child policy in 1979 to control an exponential population growth. This policy, though, has been viewed by many in the western world as an unbearable infringement of basic human rights. If, however, you think from a community perspective in which individual choices affect the community as a whole, then human rights should be associated with human responsibilities. It is amazing to me the ordeal that couples who wish to adopt have to go through. They are scrutinized to make sure they are eligible to be responsible parents. On the other hand, any teenager can have a child, and her parents and the rest of the community ending up dealing with the consequences.

Of course, I do not know what it was like to raise children in the years before I became a parent, but it seems that today, it is much harder to raise a child safely to adulthood. Yet, as we increasingly fear for our children's future, they seem to care less and less. Puberty has been starting earlier and earlier. An eight-year-old starting puberty is now not uncommon. The discrepancy between the psychological stage and the physical stage of the child makes that child a prey for sexual attention that the child does not understand. For girls in particular the change they see in their body makes them feel awkward, and that can create problems with their perception of their own body in the long run. Additionally, teenagers' social networks are more and more out of their parents' control. As a result of these larger, more diverse networks, teenagers can have a social life outside of their parent's control. Early pregnancies that we used to hear frequently happening in low-income, socially disadvantaged social groups are now happening in all social classes. In France, where the law providing free legal abortion for women who are not further along than three months in their pregnancy has been in place since 1975, and where teenagers can go on their own to specific centers called Planning Familial to get free contraception, we rarely ever heard of any teen pregnancies in certain social groups. Recently, I was told about two cases of teen pregnancy in the upper middle class in France. A 19-year-old girl who found out she was 7-and-a-half-months pregnant after having intercourse with a 17-year-old boy. Even more recently, a 14-year-old girl gave birth to a baby boy, and the father is only 15. Although anectodal, these two examples show that teen pregnancies happen in a social group that usually has the resources to be informed, and to prevent or stop the pregnancy. These examples seem to me a step backward in the movement that has been leading women to freedom. Contraception and early abortion are fundamental to women's freedom. A teenager may be able to conceive physically but we all know that psychologically she is far from ready to be a parent. I place an emphasis on the mother rather than the teenage father because, in the vast majority of cases, the consequences of the pregnancy are primarily born by the mother and her family. If we only take the fact that the pregnancy itself often leads the mother to drop out high school, the impact on the father's life is not comparable. The Centers for Disease Control and Prevention[12] states that in 2011, in the United States, *"Only about 50% of teen mothers receive a high school diploma by 22 years of age, versus approximately 90% of women who had not given birth during adolescence."* In the U.S. only, the National Campaign to Prevent Teen and Unplanned Pregnancies[13] states: *"Teen childbearing in the United States cost taxpayers (federal, state, and local) at least $10.9 billion in 2008, according to an updated analysis by The National Campaign to Prevent Teen and Unplanned Pregnancy. Most of the costs of teen childbearing are associated with negative consequences for the children of teen mothers, including increased costs for health care, foster care, incarceration, and lost tax revenue."*

If we accept the fact that the human life span is increasing, and we are aware that parenting is a lifetime commitment, we need to think about where these kids who are conceived outside of any family structure will end up. As life spans increase, the cost for the community increases as well. In addition to the religious aspects of marriage, marriage is a legal framework that protects those within it: wife, husband, and children. This legal structure makes the relationship official for everyone. All sorts of automatic rights derive

12 http://www.ezcouple.com/cdc2
13 http://www.ezcouple.com/ncptu

from this. Marriage was initially meant to give a full, unquestionable identity to the children born from that relationship, as well as giving full protection to the mother. The husband is legally the father, and the burden of proof that he is not is on anyone who would claim otherwise; the mother therefore has the right to financial support for herself and her children. Legal custody is implied, and alimonies can be asked for if the father leaves the mother. The father is also spared the need to prove his paternity.

There are more risks in having children outside of marriage than there are advantages.

First, the mother might have to track down the father to acknowledge paternity. Then, only through legal hassles will she get financial help to raise the child. In many cases she will be left to raise that child to adulthood on her own. Once the couple is married, the burden of proof shifts to the partner who contests anything. That makes a big difference for a new mom.

When you consider how difficult it is to raise balanced kids today, having two parents on the task doesn't seem like too many. Why make things more complicated when we all crave simplification?

Children coming from a dissolved marriage is the second group unprotected by their parents' marriage. A recomposed family is a family composed of parts of other broken families. What I'm arguing goes against the popular belief that recomposed families are the way to go. I disagree that they are because recomposed families make parenting more difficult by several orders of magnitude:, children quickly learn how to manipulate the adults in the family. The children rarely consider the adult who is not a blood relative an authority figure. Both adults must work daily on gaining the children's respect. Parents want to make the new family work so much that they will capitulate to the children. The parent's partner will either give into compromises as well, or face the child's immediate hostility. The primary parenting role, proper guidance, becomes increasingly difficult. We each have a limited amount of energy to deal with familial conflict. What messages get through when a child does not want to listen? Proper guidance does not necessarily meet the approval of the child; in fact it rarely does. And a parent needs energy to convince a child to follow his or her guidance. At the end of the day in particular, the energy left is limited.

Far easier than any of these adjustments, compromises, or capitulations is to make the initial relationship work in the first place: discomfort in a relationship very often reveals some personal challenges that we would be better off dealing with directly. If we can't control our partner, we have full control over changing ourselves. It takes two to be in a conflict: exploring and addressing the part we play is the best way to learn how to end the conflict.

2

WHEN IT MOSTLY COMES DOWN TO YOU

When something goes wrong, the easy road is always to blame others. When it comes to relationships, we would all profit from looking inside first: our health and our mindset have everything to do with our ability to welcome, understand, and be with someone else. We are the determining factor of what happens in our life. It is therefore critical to work on our own emotional state, and to be aware that our mind leads our life. Previously, I stated that passion is driven by self-centered desires. We are at the center of our perceptions, and so we are the only ones who can make the necessary changes to improve our wellbeing.

Part 1: Work On Your Beliefs

∽

Your mind directs your mood, and your mood affects your interactions with everyone, including your partner. Your mood is the result of your beliefs and your physiological and biochemical balance. When you have been living with someone for a long time, you are less likely to use what I would call "make-up" for the mood. And your partner is the receiver of your true mood day after day. If it is one of the wonders of a long-term relationship to be able to truly be yourself with your partner, that wonder should not become a burden for your relationship. Therefore, you should always take a close look at your own mood. If your mood is unsteady, if you feel depressed, if you feel mood swings, you should look into what might be causing them and address those causes. You may have good reasons to have negative emotions. That does not mean that you can't do anything about how you feel. In fact, the more quickly you address these feelings and improve your mood, the sooner your outside reality will change for the better. In order to have a steady mood that helps you keep your emotions in balance, you must work on two levels:

1. The beliefs that frame your perception.

2. Your physical balance.

Everything in life can be viewed positively or negatively; it is all a question of perspective. You don't have to be totally delusional to decide to see the bright side of everything. Doing so just makes your life lighter. You can decide to see and put your focus on what goes well, but if you don't want that perspective to be short-lived, you need to have the approval of your subconscious.

If you have a rather pessimistic view of things, the negative is most likely what your subconscious mind is programmed to focus on. This is your comfort zone. To change a pattern as strong as this one you need to take the risk of going outside of that zone. You need to leave that "safe" space in order to improve anything in your life. Your comfort zone is nothing less than your current reality. That means that your subconscious mind is programmed to maintain the status quo.

Why you must reprogram your subconscious mind in order to really improve your relationship in the long run? Only four to six percent of all our actions are triggered by the conscious mind. To learn more about the subconscious mind, please read this <u>article on the power of the brain</u>[14], written by John Assaraf. Assaraf is an entrepreneur in the self-improvement industry; his focus is on neuroscience and the brain's plasticity and potential. He developed a program to train the brain to achieve more. He was featured in the movie "The Secret" (2006). Whether you believe in "The Secret" or the "Law of Attraction" does not matter. What he says about the power of the brain is backed by <u>scientific research</u>[15]. In fact, Bruce H. Lipton and Steve Bhaerman in their most recent book, <u>Spontaneous Evolution: Our Positive Future and a Way to Get There From Here</u>[16], confirm the theory that our thoughts affect our brain chemistry Lipton explains this theory, derived from Napoleon Hill's ideas, of how our mind, or our ability to think affects the very biology of each cell in our body. Napoleon Hill is a journalist and author who, in 1928, published a multi-volume study titled The Law of Success: this study, which examined the most successful men at the time for over twenty years, was commissioned by Andrew Carnegie, who believed that there was a simple formula that would lead anyone who used it to success. <u>Hill's book</u>[17], reissued many times, is a fascinating way to understand the will power and the mindset of successful people. If you want to know more about cell

14 http://www.ezcouple.com/assarf
15 http://www.ezcouple.com/elsevier
16 http://www.ezcouple.com/lipton
17 http://www.ezcouple.com/Hill

biology and quantum physics, you can watch this video called The New Biology-Where Mind and Matter Meet[18]. I also recommend that you to go to nourfoundation.com[19], nongovernmental organization in special consultative status to the United Nations Economic and Social Council, to find out about the latest research on the brain, mind, and consciousness. These terms have subtle differences: the brain refers more to the physical part of the body, the mind is more the brain in action, and consciousness refers to our ability to think. Often though the three words are used interchangeably. I recommend that you do your own research to better understand this fascinating part of our body that plays such a big role in our ability to enjoy life.

My purpose here is to offer some solutions when possible. So if you are not fully satisfied with your relationship as it is, it may be time for you to change what needs to be changed...within you. You will find many brain training programs out there to teach you how to reprogram your belief system.

There are two techniques in particular that I would like to recommend. I have used them both successfully: the Emotional Freedom Technique (EFT) and Psyche-K.

These techniques are fantastic for getting any change to last effortlessly. They are easy to learn, and once you know them, you can use them on your own. They are both empowering tools for you to feel in control of your life. Deciding to change is the first step. The second step is doing it. The third and most important step is to integrate it in such a way that you don't need to consciously think about it to make it happen. The two techniques, which I explain below, are remarkable because they are no-drama techniques. It won't take you sessions and sessions that last years before you see any results. Even if you have no

18 http://www.ezcouple.com/nbio
19 http://www.ezcouple.com/nour

inclination to dig into your past through psychotherapy, you will love these two techniques. The Emotional Freedom Technique addresses negative emotions you may feel without necessarily investigating the reasons behind your feelings. It decreases the intensity of the feeling behind the emotion until the emotion is completely released. Psyche-K approaches the problem from a radically different perspective: you detail the reality as you would love to see it, and you install beliefs that support that reality as if you were installing a software. I feel the two techniques complement each other quite well.

First, **EFT: Emotional Freedom Technique**.

Emotional Freedom Technique is an acupressure tapping technique that you can easily learn and do on your own, to clear the intensity of negative emotions and allow you to move on, therefore changing your beliefs and their consequences.

I was introduced to EFT when I lived in Hong Kong. It seemed amazingly simple – even children can use it – and I decided to learn it for me and for my family. I bought all the training DVDs that Gary Craig, the founder, had produced and became an EFT practitioner. I practiced it on everyone who was willing to give it a try. While I was working at The Body Group[20], a fantastic healing clinic in Hong Kong, as a Nambudripad Allergy Elimination Technique (NAET) practitioner – NAET is also an acupressure technique that aims to relieve allergies – and EFT practitioner, I witnessed the major and rapid improvements EFT demonstrated with chronic diseases of all sorts.

There is no scientific explanation yet about what makes EFT so efficient in addressing any problem linked to emotions and pain, but it works. It also works as an amazing emergency technique that can prevent Post-Traumatic Stress Disorder (PTSD). It is therefore

---

20 http://www.ezcouple.com/bdg

also useful to address fear after any traumatic event. In the case of a traumatic event, you may need several rounds of ten tapping sequences to tackle the negative emotion, but you will eventually release it. The most impressive healings I witnessed while practicing EFT ranged from curing a spider phobia and ending severe chronic back pain to eliminating long-term anger and sadness due to life events. An hour-long session was enough to deal with the spider phobia. The severe back pain took three sessions, and I believe that it could have been done more quickly if I had had more experience in guiding the sessions. Chronic anger was more challenging because it is an emotion that can have so many roots, but it was solved within two weeks of two full hours of tapping. Please watch <u>my video on Youtube</u>[21] where I demonstrate the tapping sequence and explain how you can use EFT for children. If you Google "Emotional Freedom Technique," you will find tons of more or less accurate information. Make sure to check <u>emofree.com</u>[22], Gary Craig's website. Craig is the founder of EFT as it is today, and he is a man of great integrity. He has never pretended to be the inventor of EFT, or a doctor. Neither has he ever promised clients the world and beyond. Check out his website to learn EFT for yourself; he has released an in-depth online EFT tutorial. You can also have a look at this YouTube video featuring Gary Craig helping a lady who had a blood disorder: it is called "<u>Lynn's Blood Fatigue</u>"[23], and it clearly shows how EFT affects your blood cells.

So, how might you use EFT in your relationship? Well, EFT can really be helpful any time you feel frustration, annoyance, anger, or other negative emotion towards your partner. If you work on regulating your own feelings first, you will be much more efficient in communicating to your partner what triggered the negative feeling

---

21 http://www.ezcouple.com/vid2

22 http://www.ezcouple.com/eft

23 http://www.ezcouple.com/vid3

in the first place. Emotional outbursts rarely convey effectively one's message.

So, how can you employ EFT to improve your relationship?

To begin, you must grade your negative emotion on a scale of 0 to 10, 10 being the most acute version of that feeling.

Then, start tapping, respecting the sequence while you repeat a sentence. Check how you feel, and tap again until you reach 0.

Try to be precise in articulating how you feel. The more precise you are, the sooner you will feel better.

See the sentences below as examples of what you might say while you tap: choose one that resonates the most with you.

Even though I am really annoyed when my partner does (be as specific as possible), *I deeply love and accept myself.*

Even if I am hurt when my partner talks to me that way, I deeply love and accept myself.

Even though I am really tired of listening to my partner, I deeply love and accept myself.

Whatever sentences you create, be sure that you start with an "I" sentence: you want to work on your own emotions to release them.

Even if his mess drives me nuts, for example, should be rephrased as *Even if I feel upset, angry…each time I see his mess, I deeply love and accept myself.*

If your emotions are so overwhelming that you feel you can't handle this on your own, contact an EFT practitioner. You can find one through emofree.com. I recommend Michelle Hardwick, based in the UK. She is an amazing healer, and she combines different techniques with EFT to help you achieve your goal faster. You can work with her via Skype from your home. Check her site[24] she is as amazing as her smile.

---

24 http://www.ezcouple.com/michelle

The second technique is **Psyche-K**.

I was introduced to Psyche-K a few years ago, and I have been amazed by the results everybody gets with this technique. It is not as easy to learn as EFT can be, but it is fun to do. Psyche uses a sequence of movements meant to stimulate both hemispheres of the brain in order to integrate an affirmation that you choose. Kinesiology, or the muscle response from the body, helps determine the necessity and the type of sequence of movement that will successfully install a new belief. Kinesiology is used to communicate with the subconscious mind. The sequences of possible movement are very easy to perform. One time is usually enough to properly install a new belief via a clear affirmation. On the spot, you will not notice much difference, but if you observe your reactions in the days and weeks that follow, you will note a change in your perceptions of everything linked to the new belief. With Psyche-K, you have the opportunity to easily change your preconceived ideas about relationships that limit your ability to enjoy your life. Your ideas of division of roles for instance, might need an upgrade. Spousonomics[25], a book written by Paula Szuchman and Jenny Anderson, offers an interesting perspective that may challenge your beliefs about roles in relationships. Sex is another field where you would be better off assessing your beliefs. We all have intense beliefs regarding sex, about what is right and what is wrong, about who should initiate things and how. Pause for a moment and ask yourself what you would love your sexuality with your partner to be like. Be specific. Write it down to make sure you don't forget any details. That technique, by the way, is called visualization.

To learn more about Psyche-K, you can watch Rob Williams's video, called "Rob Williams Explains Why PSYCHE-K Works."[26] Even if

---

25 http://www.ezcouple.com/spouso
26 http://www.ezcouple.com/vid4

you don't believe in the spiritual part of Rob Williams's explanation, Psyche-K can help you with your relationship.

You can learn the first level of Psyche-K over a two-day workshop. But if your time is limited, just find a practitioner through Psyche-K. com[27]. If you happen to be in Southern California, Karen Johnson[28] is professional, dedicated, efficient, and fun to work with.

These two techniques, EFT and Psyche-K, are not conventional and may be unknown or disregarded by the medical establishment. What matters, though, is you: there is no risk or side effect to trying them out. If one or both of them works, do you really care about the fact that most people don't know about them? Perseverance and a willingness to change are the keys to achieving any type of success. When we adjust to the environment, we can persevere. Life is fulfilling if we accept the idea of change. Change is the necessary way to grow. To improve our life, we must be willing to take risks to reach the next step. We all do that in various parts of our lives, but we tend to forget to do it in our most important relationship.

Part 2: Keep Nutrient Deficiencies At Bay

For a long time I believed that only emotions were influencing my mood. I thought that emotion patterns were the result of trauma that only a psychological approach could heal. Well, that was far from the truth.

Traumas cause a physiological reaction within the body that impairs its ability to function properly. While a psychological approach may be necessary in many cases, it is never enough. A perfect example of this is

27 http://www.ezcouple.com/psyk
28 http://www.ezcouple.com/karen

an allergic reaction: most allergies have an emotional root cause. Once the emotional origin of the allergy is dealt with, it often disappears. It is not rare that EFT or Psyche-K alone solves chronic pain for that reason. However, someone who has had severe allergies for a long time will have a deficient immune system and nutritional deficiencies because the body no longer properly absorbs vitamins and minerals. Its ability to identify what is good and what is bad becomes distorted. I was severely allergic as a child and ended up in the emergency care unit twice. I remember carrying a shot of cortisone with me any time I went on a trip. By the time I was 30 I had developed many allergies. As an adult, I used kinesiology to identify what I was initially allergic to. I used Nambudripad Allergy Elimination Technique (NAET)[29] and EFT to get rid of all my allergies. I must say though that I needed many, many NAET sessions to achieve that. I tend to think that I would have healed more quickly had Andrea Schropel handled the treatment. Based in Germany, Andrea is an MD specializing in neuro-biochemistry. She is in charge of English-language NAET training throughout the world, as well as NAET Europe.

Despite good eating habits and a healthy lifestyle, even if you are not allergic, you need extra vitamins and minerals to bring your body back into balance. Our contemporary lifestyle increases the oxidation process, therefore impairing our health. Minerals in the soils are depleted; shelf time of fresh produce is too long, and most food is cooked, with no vitamins left from the cooking process. There is no way you can fight that with daily meals, even organic ones. The right supplements limit the damage done to your cells. Only a good holistic doctor will be able to clearly identify what your body is lacking and orchestrate a nutritional therapy tailor-made for you. Additionally, stress accelerates aging and only lifestyle changes and the right

29 http://www.ezcouple.com/naet

supplements can reverse that process. If you live a stressful life, and who does not these days, you need to be aware that oxidation processes within your body are accelerated. I take a regimen of vitamins and minerals updated every six months or more often if I feel the need for it, following my doctor's suggestions. Food is not as simple as it used to be. Toxins have increased considerably, and it takes extra help to make sure one reaches optimum health. However, there is a debate over whether or not we should take supplements because many people self-medicate when it comes to supplements. These people are unaware of the potential interactions these supplements might have with their doctor-prescribed medication. Supplements have active ingredients that may do wonders for your health if they are rightly targeted, but professional advice is usually required to do so. Specialists define through specific tests what exactly is needed to avoid deficiencies. Holistic doctors are usually very knowledgeable on the various kinds of supplements available. I believe that we all need supplements, but we don't all need the same ones in the same dosage. Between processed foods, the shelf life of fresh produce, pollution, and stress levels, rare are those who don't need any supplements. Deficiencies lead to various symptoms. One of them can be mood swings. Female mood swings can be caused by progesterone deficiency. Premenstrual Syndrome (PMS) can be a nightmare for the whole family, and the male partner in particular. Mood swings in stressed men are very often aggravated by vitamin B deficiencies, B6 and B12 in particular.

Not all supplements are created equal, and certain brands are better than others. Better means efficient. And cheap is rarely a good sign. It is hard to go wrong with Metagenics. I have noticed, for example, that vitamin C from Metagenics is far more efficient than any other over-the-counter brand to take to prevent an incipient cold. Note that

I found my wonderful doctor through their website[30]. If you live in Europe or in Asia, you can easily get Biocare[31], it is a reliable brand, too. Also know that food based vitamins are easily absorbed and that may not be the case with synthetic vitamins.

If you need one more motivation to act on identifying and addressing any deficiencies now, you should know that these nutrients not only increase your energy level but they also increase your libido. So, don't wait for back pain, or an ache here and there to start taking care of your body.

A healthy mind in a healthy body gives you enough energy to deal with everything...including your relationship. Of course, supplements are not miracle pills; they will not replace a healthy diet. And they won't do much if you don't eat healthfully in the first place. When you are in a relationship, eating healthfully can prove to be very challenging. I address this in detail in Chapter 7, Part 3. Again, any change has to start with you taking care of your own health first. Seeing your own health improve may be the best motivation for your partner to join you in that journey.

Health is first an individual road because eating is so emotionally charged that any change has to be willingly adopted.

Part 3: Boost Your Energy With A Healthful Diet

Our natural state is one of health, so we tend to take health for granted, forgetting how critical it is in our life. A flu that traps you in bed for several days is usually a good reminder that health is a prerequisite for life. When you are sick, the world revolves around the

---

30 http://www.ezcouple.com/vit1
31 http://www.ezcouple.com/vit2

illness, and all your energy is dedicated to healing.

The body is a fascinating machine, amazingly sophisticated, and marvelously orchestrated. It is the home for our soul. Assuming that we begin life in a healthy state, and even this is less and less the case in the western world, the challenge is to stay healthy. Doing so is a daily commitment with the immediate gratification of feeling vibrant. In a vibrant body, our mind can then guide us without restriction. Unfortunately, very few people know what true health is: in fact, most people live with aches and pains here and there indicating a body dysfunction that may lead to a disease, unaware of the limitations these impose on their lives. Where do you find the energy to nurture your relationship if your own energy is unnaturally limited?

Health starts with healthful food. The word "healthy" is so charged now that when it is associated with food, it almost becomes a political statement. Not so long ago our family had a friend over, and I offered him a green smoothie we often make. I gave him a small glass of the green drink. After the first sip, he said, "This is not healthy! This is good!" I realized then that people associate healthful food with disgusting and boring food. There is no joy, fun, or pleasure in eating healthfully. Yet it is actually the opposite! Eating healthfully means enjoying a variety of tastes and flavors that makes eating a journey. Eating is the beginning of discovering various food and taste sensations. When you eat healthfully, eating becomes meaningful.

Unfortunately, many people have dropped all interest in the way they eat, perceiving meal time as a waste of time. However, meals are an opportunity for connections at a very deep level. Eating healthfully does take more time and money than it does when you don't care about what you're eating. Nothing beats the speed and cost of a Big Mac meal from a drive-through lane. Check out this interesting article from The Atlantic, "Cheap Eats: How America Spends Money on Food,"[32] which includes the most recent statistics on our food and eating habits. Do you find it surprising that the average household in the US spends less than 14 percent of their income on food when food is the determining factor in their health? By contrast, in 1900, food was close to 40 percent of a household's total spending.[33] And while food prices have gradually lowered since then, it is not enough to account for the ridiculously low proportion allocated to our body fuel.

Our priorities today make no sense. In two generations we have lost some very important knowledge, critical to our survival: how to prepare food to eat. If we want healthful eating to spread and become the norm, more than spending more money on food itself, we need to educate people. We must teach people how to turn fresh produce into palatable food. I feel blessed to come from a culture that has always placed a strong emphasis on meals and the value of the connections you can have with people around a table of great food. Our lives are so busy however, that even the French often choose the easy road of processed and fast food… In France too, alarm bells are ringing. You see, France has an extensive welfare system that has been in serious trouble for the past twenty years, and this system can't cope with the growing rate of illnesses that require heavy treatments. So France has recently made healthful eating a national priority.

At an individual level it usually takes a more or less dramatic wakeup call to make us change. In theory, we know it is rather sensible to eat healthfully, but it never really sinks in until we get a good scare. Humankind is not that good at prevention.

I was no different. Despite the fact that on my father's side everybody died from cancer, I had the boldness youth gave me, thinking that

---

32 http://www.ezcouple.com/atl13
33 http://www.ezcouple.com/bsw080213

nothing would ever happen to me. Luckily, I have never had a sweet tooth, so the damage has not been too hard to repair. Even so, major symptoms raised my awareness when I was 33 and living in Singapore. I started to have a low-grade fever, and I felt somewhere between tired to exhausted most of the day. I went to see my regular doctor, who sent me to a doctor specialist in internal medicine. She ordered a blood test, a urine test, an endoscopy, and colonoscopy, knowing that my father had died from colon cancer. After the procedure, the gastroenterologist she recommended asked to meet us both, my husband and me, and his first words were that he had hardly ever seen so many different issues in a person my age. What worried him most was a polyp that he had removed during the colonoscopy: he suspected cancer. It was a Friday and we were supposed to have the results of the biopsy on Monday. My husband and I then spent the worst weekend of our lives. We both knew what cancer at 33 meant in terms of life expectancy, and we were devastated at the prospect. When it turned out that the polyp was not cancerous, that all the white dots spread along the wall of my colon were nothing serious known to doctors, and that the wall mutation on the lower part of my esophagus would remain a risk, the relief was huge!

But I still had the same symptoms, in addition to this esophagus wall mutation to keep an eye on. I was scheduled for a full examination again in six months. The specialist in internal medicine, who had seen the beginning of an autoimmune disease in the blood test, sent me to a rheumatologist who did further tests. He couldn't identify the source of my autoimmune disease. It wasn't lupus, and it wasn't rheumatoid arthritis, for which he had no cure anyway... I went back to my internist, who looked at me and said, "Look, I could give you antibiotics to see if they'll help, but I don't think it will do much; I have nothing to offer you. If I were you, I would go see a naturopath."

I was grateful for her honesty and followed her advice.

When I saw the naturopath, he did some weird tests, having me hold different vials in one hand and a metal mass in the other hand. He used a German machine to do all these tests. Right after completing the tests, he said that I was invaded by Candida albicans (a fungal overgrowth in the intestinal track that causes yeast infections), and that I needed to go on a strict diet in order to start a detoxification. After the cancer scare, I was ready to do anything, and laughed at the idea of a 12-day diet. He warned me, though, that it could be extremely painful for the first few days, and that I should not stop the diet until all pain was gone. The diet was simple: eggs, steamed fish, lean white meat, olive oil, and plenty of green vegetables. Nothing else! When you eat this type of diet, you realize how wonderful it is to be able to eat everything. But my motivation to feel better was strong. My beloved husband, who was deeply concerned, said that he would do the diet with me to help me. If THIS is not an act of love, I don't know what is. Try to stay on this diet for a few days, and you will understand what commitment it meant.

At the same time, I had to take a high dosage of olive leaf extract. And I had to have a dreadful enema every day. The first day was okay, but the second day I woke up with an unbearable headache. I called the naturopath, Mr. ND, in despair, and he said to drink more water and wait. He said not to take pain medication because it would impair the detoxification process. It was so difficult to cope with the pain that I would have stopped the diet if my husband had not motivated me to continue. The third day was just as bad, and in addition I was losing weight: by the fourth day I had lost close to five kilos (ten pounds), and believe me, I did not need to lose any weight! Mr. ND kept saying that I was losing toxins, and that was good. By the fifth day my fever was gone, and the headache was gradually going away. By the sixth day, the headache was gone. By the seventh day, I felt in shape like I had never felt before. Despite the fact that my food regimen was green beans and a hard-boiled egg in the morning, fish and green salad with no dressing for lunch, and chicken and spinach for dinner, my energy level had never been so high. On the tenth day, he told me I could stop the diet, and we had a long discussion about a new diet in order to maintain my health.

This is when all of my family started to take supplements and eat organic food.

When I did the esophagogastroduodenoscopy (wish me luck for the audiobook!) combined with the colonoscopy a couple of months later, the gastroenterologist asked to meet us again after the procedure. This time it was to convey his astonishment that everything was perfectly normal, including the esophagus. His words were: "I have never seen a mutation go back to normal, especially in six months." Unfortunately he would not believe that a simple diet combined with olive leaf extract could have done the job. Today, when I think about this period of my life, I am deeply grateful. I feel blessed to have learnt early on how food matters on the path to health, and most importantly, my heart overflows with love when I think of what my husband did for me. Every day he would come back from work to have a quick lunch with me to make sure I would stay on the diet. His support has been invaluable, and I can never thank him enough for that.

This was the start of my learning how to reach optimum health. I had already read a lot about various diseases. When my father struggled with cancer and eventually died from it, although much later than doctors thought he would, I had read several books on the latest findings about cancer and its treatments. My first son and his early intestinal problems led me to investigate further about the nutrition for newborns and the impact of the first years' diet on the digestive system. My interest in health and healing processes deepened with this event. I was then determined to understand the wonderful balance that leads to health. I have never stopped learning, and I can assure you that the food we eat matters tremendously to our overall wellbeing. In fact, a proper diet can heal even the most incurable disease. For an example, please watch this Tedx Talk with Dr. Terry Wahls[34], who cured herself of multiple sclerosis by changing her diet and lifestyle.

The lack of awareness in the U.S. about the importance of what we eat in fostering health is a true mystery for me. One of the things I love about Americans is that they are so self-reliant. Any time a catastrophe happens, the whole nation mobilizes to help. The resistance to gun control, for example, which is very difficult to understand from a European perspective, shows the fierce determination to refuse to delegate one's own safety to the community. Why is it then that Americans blindly trust the medical and pharmaceutical industries, and the food industry, delegating their health to big businesses? Don't be fooled by the fact that the Food and Drug Administration (FDA) and the United States Department of Agriculture (USDA) monitor these industries. Both are useful and valuable institutions, but they have all the flaws of any large institution burdened by bureaucracy. They check what is brought to their attention following their strict requirements, and only what is brought to their attention. As a result, a costly protocol leads to FDA approval, and claims against a product have to be heavily documented before it is withdrawn from the market. The proceedings, initially meant to give a clear and legal process for anyone to follow, have become cost-prohibitive for small entities. It is not clear that this cost driven approach serves the best interest of the public.

34 http://www.ezcouple.com/vid5

Do you seriously think that if any doctor discovered a natural cure for cancer outside the current research protocols of the medical profession, that he or she could afford the costly process of FDA approval? And why would the doctor do it anyway? First, he or she would be discredited by the whole very-lucrative current cancer-related medical establishment. Think about how many people make a living on cancer diagnosis and treatments: if cancer all of sudden disappeared, a whole industry would disappear as well. So, he or she had rather heal his or her patients, and let the word spread, not too far, not too quickly, in order to avoid trouble. If an alternative medicine truly cures a disease without the side effects of drug usage, for the FDA to approve that technique, it needs multiple data given by clinical trials that follow a protocol defined by the FDA. This protocol is expensive and "can be sponsored by an organization such as a pharmaceutical company, a federal agency." (www.fda.gov)[35] Who has the most money to "sponsor" these trials? Why would any drug company sponsor a clinical trial for any technique or product outside their patent scope, and risk losing the benefits of a drug already on the market? Does that make any business sense?

Take the research on stem cells as an example. In 2009, Doris Taylor, then-professor at the University of Minnesota, made, with her team, the astonishing discovery that a dead pig's heart could beat again after an injection of stem cells cultured in a specific supportive environment for them to grow into heart cells. Stem cells have two characteristics: they have the potential to self-duplicate and divide, and they can grow into any organ. The stem cells used in research laboratories are cells taken from unused fertilized eggs when the actual cell division has occurred fewer than one hundred times. Can you imagine the healing potential of being able to bring back to life

35 http://www.ezcouple.com/fda

a dying organ? Taylor received letters and letters from parents and children who have a loved one suffering from a severe disease. They want their loved one to be part of the clinical trials when possible. Her discovery is major, and yet had you heard about it? Listen to her conversation with Krista Tippett, "Stem Cells: Untold Stories,"[36] on NPR's podcast "Krista Tippet On Being." The humility, beauty, and spirituality behind this woman's work will stun you. You can also watch Great Conversations: Innovative Science[37], recorded in April of 2009, on YouTube in which Doris Taylor is interviewed by Dr. Patricia Simmons. Watch until the end, the best is there. These two scientists are incredible.

You and I have little control over the flaws of a system that has lost track of its initial goal. What we can control, however, is what we put in our mouth, what type of food we buy. No one else has more interest in our health than we do: our aches and pains feed a whole system outside of us, but these aches and pains hinder our lives, and limit our capacity to be.

The choice is ours, for us, and for our children. The information is everywhere; all you need is an internet connection. You might learn interesting facts about nutrition and behavior[38] that will invite you to adjust your own diet. You will also learn that grass-fed and grain-fed red meats are not equal in either nutritional value or ease of digestion, grass-fed meat being best.[39] You will then understand why a ketogenic diet, a diet based on a high amount of quality protein and beneficial fat, and a low-carbohydrate intake, is so successful with serious conditions including cancer, even though you may not have heard about it.

---

36 http://www.ezcouple.com/nprob
37 http://www.ezcouple.com/vid6
38 http://www.ezcouple.com/crim
39 http://www.ezcouple.com/nutri

Vibrant health is more than a choice; it is the mindful way to be. Ultimately our health is in our hands. Do your own research, and make an informed decision. From the perspective of being in a relationship, what grounds would justify imposing on others the consequences of neglecting our own body? Supporting someone sick is extremely difficult. A time will come when we are liable for the consequences of our poor diet choices. As science defines more closely what nourishes the cells of the body and what depletes them, knowingly eating what damages the body will eventually be a liability, especially if the rest of the community has to pay for it. For now it only burdens the life of your loved one.

3

LEARN TO BE EFFICIENT
WHEN IT COMES TO LOVE

L ove and efficiency are rarely combined. Thinking of love in
terms of efficiency may not sound romantic. Yet, do we have
time to afford inefficiency in any area of our life? Not so long ago, the
pace of life was much, much slower, and we could afford to waste time.
Now we can't. Being inefficient in your relationship might result in
your partner leaving you. Days are still only twenty-four hours long,
and our physical need for sleep remains as it has always been. And
yet the number of things to accomplish in a day has never been so
high. Therefore, we have to think from a goal-oriented perspective:
achieving those goals depends on efficiency. The goal here is the
mutual satisfaction of both persons in a relationship, so they can both

reach a greater level of love, trust and respect. That is no easy task in our world, where individualism is preponderant. If we want somebody else to feel our love, we had better make sure we show it.

Part 1: Show Your Love So It Is Felt

One of the biggest misleading assumptions about love today is that it is innate. Religions and spiritual guides keep repeating that we are all creatures of love, implying that we must therefore all know how to love. In reality however, we need very good lessons before we are able to love in the deep sense of the word. Just observe two-year-olds together in a playground to see how human kindness and love spontaneously show in their interactions. Two-year-olds have very little sense of self beyond their ego. Ego is linked to survival, not to respect, and not to love. Love belongs to a higher stage of consciousness and being. With maturity come various levels of consciousness that keep the ego under control. However, even as adults, going beyond the ego does not come naturally; the adult world is filled with magnificent egos walking around. Love needs to be felt, learned, and taught.

Couples wrongly assume that the initial magic in their relationship will last forever, and they wrongly believe that it is this magic that is love. So once passion has waned, it can be hard to understand what we are doing wrong. We don't feel that we are any different. In fact, we are not much different. What has changed is that what was cute, funny, and romantic, through the blind eyes of passion, can now be childish, exasperating, and pathetic. The incompetence at a chore or a task may be funny and endearing at first, but it may turn annoying after a while. Our partner's perception of us is not as forgiving anymore, triggering our own insecurity. To make us feel good about our self again, our desire for love becomes so intense that we will do anything we can in order to show how much we care…but we will do it our way.

The miscommunication and frustration in long-term relationships very often stem from the fact that we love the other the way we want to be loved. That specific way of loving that we desire is a combination of beliefs inherited or acquired, and our own sense of pleasure. Our desire for pleasure is very intense, and it motivates our gestures towards others with the unconscious hope that we will get the expected pleasure in return. If you are lucky enough to be with someone who shares with you his or her language of love, your task is easier, but you still have to come to terms with your respective beliefs.

So, efficiently loving another human being starts with knowing what makes that person feel loved. I highly recommend that you read, if you haven't yet, Gary Chapman's book on the five love languages[40]. This best-selling book should be given to everyone during pre-marriage counseling. It should be read at the beginning of any relationship meant to last. Even if it does not deal with your beliefs, it helps you identify your partner's love language and your own. You then have a path to follow if you want to show your love so it is felt.

Most relationships degrade slowly, with subtle signs along the way that are very often ignored. One mistake we all make at one point or another is to assume that our partner knows how much we love him or her. Regular confirmations are badly needed by both partners. We should not presume he or she knows how we feel. Very often we feel love but we don't show it, forgetting that what we feel is not necessarily clear to our partner. We should choose a simple way to regularly tell our partner how much we love him or her, even if we feel it is obvious. We should not feel shy or embarrassed. We should not try to make it light either. Saying "I love you" to anyone is profound and meaningful.

---

40 http://www.ezcouple.com/5ll

It triggers heart felt emotions, and we should allow ourselves to feel that love pouring out of our heart. This simple gesture will be special for us and for the person who receives it.

Let me add here a moving poem from the 14th century Persian author named Hafez. I was blessed to learn about this poem through Father Greg Boyle's voice on Krista Tippet's[41] wonderful radio show "On Being."

"With That Moon Language"
Admit something:
Everyone you see, you say to them,
"Love me."
Of course you do not do this out loud;
Otherwise,
Someone would call the cops.
Still though, think about this,
This great pull in us to connect.
Why not become the one
Who lives with a full moon in each eye?
That is always saying
With that sweet moon
Language
What every other eye in this world
Is dying to
Hear.

The pace of our lives does not leave much spare time, and we tend to optimize on all levels, including our conversations, our gestures, and our actions. If this definitely makes sense as a coping mechanism in some areas of our lives, with our life partner, it can be devastating. We can be efficient when it comes to a relationship without the rationalization optimization usually implies: it means making the right move at the right pace, at the right time. And it may also mean

---

41 http://www.ezcouple.com/nprob2

repeating the same move beyond rational understanding of this repetition. Let's face the fact that when it comes to affirmations of love, rationalizing the number of times you express your love would lead to use a general rule of thumb of the average number of times love should be declared in order for the other person to remember. For the one who declares his or her love that may be fine, but the other, according to his or her own state of mind, may need much more. It is not so much the knowing that matters here it is the feeling that expression of love triggers. We all want to feel loved, and we want to be sure of it. So, we like to hear love messages again and again. "Don't you know by now?" does not work... for the receiver. The more time we spend with someone, the harder it gets to offer love affirmations because our daily routines do not foster love and romance. While habits are wonderful because they relax the mind, and we don't need to think things through, they can be terrible for any relationship. Just think about the fact that we all have highs and lows according to our own schedule. When we have a bad day, this is the time we most need to feel loved. Feeling loved can turn our mood from bad to good regardless of other factors. The problem is that, very often, our lows do not make us particularly loveable: we are cranky, sad, and irritable – in other words, negative. Well, this is exactly when true love should step in. Imagine what it would feel like if your partner came to you when you were that cranky, irritable shadow of yourself and held you while saying how much he or she loves you. Wouldn't that make a big difference? It would certainly give you the opportunity to see yourself with loving eyes at a time when you are unable to do so by yourself.

This is an invaluable gift that we all deserve to receive.

We should never presume that our partner knows how much we care and love him or her just because we are here day after day. We should tell our partner, kiss our partner, and hold our partner tightly and lovingly on a regular basis. This should be a routine. It will make a difference for our partner, and eventually for us.

Who else loves us enough to go beyond our dark side? Our mother?

Do you still wonder why I claim that your long-term relationship is your biggest asset? However much there is in your bank account, whichever position you hold in your work place, in your community, nothing can fill your heart like the unconditional love that your partner can give you.

Unconditional love is the only fuel for a long-time run.

It may require some work to understand how your life partner needs to feel loved. In the process of coming to understand it however, you might learn a lot about yourself. There are great benefits in understanding that which is different.

Part 2: The Point Of Understanding That Which Is Different

Our body is programmed to reject that which is different unless it is identified and processed. Our mind is no different. Processing means that we have enough understanding of what defines the other. Many problems between men and women come from preconceived ideas we have about the other gender. These ideas are either formed after very superficial observation, or they come from outdated concepts carried over from previous generations. Feminists have served the cause of women in many ways by raising awareness of the unfair treatment of most women, and fighting to improve women's freedom and independence. These fights still have relevance in lots of places throughout the world. However it seems that the Western world is ready for a new approach, one that is less belligerent. Traditional feminism is based on a direct comparison of treatment between men and women, mainly in the work force. Often it consists in fighting for women against men. I don't think that this type of feminism is now the right road to achieve the reconciliation beneficial to both men and women. In many countries abusive behavior towards women is still rampant, but I believe that unfairness will cease when both genders have a clear understanding of the other. They will then be able to manage their expectations and their fears. Confrontation is very popular because it gives a false sense of belonging: you are either for or against something, defined by your position in a very black and white situation. But confrontation leads nowhere sustainable in the long run; we all know that reality is more in the shades of grey rather than either black or white. When two groups oppose each other, peace comes with the supremacy and dominance of one group over the other; it does not lead to mutual satisfaction. The current situation women and men experience today gives them equal access to financial independence: even if women still resist embracing the opportunities offered to them in the business world, it is only a matter of time before complete independence is achieved for them. This is a factor that will transform the nature of any long-term relationship. If we keep a warlike position in considering both genders, we will divide and eventually marginalize loving long-term, cross-gender relationships. A warlike approach is the easy route, though: rejection and victimization are the choices of those who don't want to go further, who don't want to understand the complexity of the world we live in. The real road, the one that leads us to grow into better people, goes through making space for the unknown, making space and accepting that which is different.

Accepting what is different makes us better people because we gain a better understanding of ourselves through broader perspectives. We get a better sense of the big picture, the one that goes way beyond us. This big picture is reality. Whether we like it or not, we are all interconnected to an extent that we don't ever contemplate. Globalization is one realization of this interconnectedness. The more we raise our awareness, the less scary this interconnectedness becomes. A long-term relationship will collapse if one or both stop trying to understand the other.

Earlier, I mentioned that the goal of this section is learning to manage your expectations and fears. If expectations are clear, fears may not be. So many attitudes are just the result of fear: fear of losing control, fear of not being loved, fear of being betrayed, fear of being alone, and so on.

Fears only come from imagination and anticipation. Imagination roots into our beliefs system that we wrongly assume to be knowledge. Beliefs are static: they are based on collective and personal memory. Collective memory is often confused with our cultural traits when it is based on these traits and past events. The collective memory I am referring to here encompasses the family memory as well. The collective memory has been responsible for many wars in Europe where nations such as France and Great Britain would fight over and over throughout the centuries. This memory is extremely powerful in forming our perspective. The world evolves constantly, as well as we, human beings, do; men and women are different from what they were yesterday and different from what they will be tomorrow. Therefore, we should always question our beliefs to make sure they are up-to-date.

Unconsciously, I chose a life where my beliefs would constantly be challenged. Even if I find it sometimes difficult and unsettling, I would not want another life. It is absolutely fascinating to see that the revered scientific theory about relativity applies everywhere to everyone. Reputation and credentials you have here may have little or no value there. What matters there does not matter here. So, we should never presume we know, we should always be curious, and we should expect to change.

Many men fear they will lose their soul or their virility if they explore the female world. What they don't understand is that there is a female part in every male: if they investigate and better understand their female side, not only will they improve their relationship with all women, but they will also have a better understanding of themselves. They will discover tools they did not suspect they had. Women, by necessity, do not have the same reluctance, and they have explored the male side through the business world. Despite this, many women have failed to draw the right conclusions when it comes to their approach with their male partner. They wrongly return to thinking that they're supposed to be a fragile creature who loves the protection of the man. Femininity is associated with fragility and a need for protection. Women, for a start, should stop associating femininity with weakness.

The preponderance of the business world still follows male rules: not only are men still mostly in charge, but communication is very masculine, and vision and management also follow a male mindset in most organizations. However, more and more women are reaching the top, bringing their own perspective in the process. The years to come will see these rules reviewed, reconsidered, and eventually changed. I know how important it is for men to feel powerful; so these upcoming changes may look frightening, but the truth is that the nature of their power will change, not the fact that men have power. The shift will be from absolute power to controlled power. Absolute power is a solitary exercise that underestimates the benefit of other people's inputs. This type of power may or may not take into account other people's opinions. Controlled power, on the other hand, can't afford to ignore others' reality: the power is kept and respected as long as it serves a purpose agreed upon by a majority. Absolute power fosters competition, greed, selfishness, and, most importantly, imbalance. Controlled power, on the contrary, works for the benefit of the whole community: it nurtures ethics and healthy competition for innovation. Besides, women do not seek power. They want to feel special, really special. They want to make a difference. If they have the possibility of being listened to and recognized without reaching out for power, they will not even challenge men for power. A balanced couple is a good example on a smaller scale of true collaboration between a man and a woman. In a balanced couple, we can see all the wonderful benefits everybody in the family gets from this kind of collaboration. It is important to challenge our beliefs, whatever they are, and install, if we need to, new beliefs that will support our life and our relationship better.

We all need to learn to navigate in the depths of the female side: this is where true creativity stems from.

When we consider gender characteristics, it is important to understand them and work on them when they hinder our communication with the other gender. Let me highlight one characteristic in particular that deserves our attention: women's indecisiveness. One of the hardest tasks for a woman is to know exactly what she wants. She is adamant and can talk forever about what she does not want, but very often, when she is asked bluntly what she does want, there is a blank. Of course she is not indecisive about everything in life, but it is particularly true with her expectations regarding her life partner. I have always wondered why this is so. I finally came up with the beginning of an explanation that I would love to share with you:

Two inherited collective beliefs are at play here.

1. A woman is asked; she does not ask.

2. Saying precisely what she wants is the last resort in her way of communicating.

If you are older than twenty, please know she has totally lost respect for you by the time she has said explicitly what she wants. The way women communicate is subtle, even if there are many more conversations in their interactions than there are for the opposite gender. We women can't help but think that there is something vulgar and despicable in being precise and detailed in a request. We mistakenly believe that evolved human beings should understand, without words, simply by caring enough. Isn't that what we are supposed to do during pregnancy for the child we will bear and for the few months after its birth? For a little over a year, we are guessing about what the baby needs, and during this time, we are supposed to guess right. Our guesses must answer critical questions: Does the child move normally? Is he okay? The baby is crying, what does it mean? These are not casual questions, and yet, we manage to answer them well enough! So when we see that the garbage can is full, we really wonder who the dummy is that does not see that the garbage bag needs to be changed! This is not rocket science, is it? Should we place a beeping sign on it, saying "Garbage full, new bag needed"? Whether consciously or not this is how we women feel.

But the truth is elsewhere.

The truth of how we feel lies in our differences. Men are not programmed to bear a child for nine months and respond to its basic needs right after birth. Although you don't need to go through the process of pregnancy and breastfeeding to develop your intuition, what is true though is that this process forces you to develop it.

Men do not have that opportunity. Of course in the process of seduction, all a man's energy is dedicated to you, ladies, so you assume that they can guess what you want. The reality, though, is that they don't. They just apply the same recipe learned from generation to generation, where they talk nicely, they compliment, they spend time, as much as they can, and they are careful in their physical approach. This recipe has never failed, but the success initially achieved is temporary, because this energy-consuming strategy is not sustainable in the long run. Very quickly men turn back to what they truly are, just like we, women, do. In all fairness, we are never as funny, as easy going, as forgiving, as sexy, or as charming as when we are seducing a man or being seduced.

So what to do about this difference in our guessing abilities?

We women want things to be done properly, and more importantly we want to feel special in our relationship. This is the goal that we should aim to reach with pragmatism. By the way, since men excel at pragmatism, it is not a bad idea to ask them advice about that part. Let's pause for one second: Ladies, have you ever wished that you could read or listen to somebody telling you exactly what to do with your newborn baby? For those of you who have forgotten, please close your eyes and tune into that moment when you were holding your newborn baby who was crying to make you deaf, and you had no clue what to do with him or her. If you are not in total denial, you felt hopeless then. At least, I felt that way; and I was reading everything under the sun, becoming even more confused, because very few people agree about how to take care of crying newborns. So, in the end, I relied on my intuition, which grew more and more reliable, but whether it was my intuition or my relying on it, it never came naturally to me.

Even if women are programmed for guessing, they are not expert at it, and it takes time and practice to become a good guesser. Why on earth do we expect that ability from men? We have to go through that process because it's the way things are meant to be; they don't, for the same reason. Guessing well eventually becomes a huge asset that we can leverage, and one would think that men would be better off learning it, too. They might, but for now they don't. Similarly, we would gain a lot in learning from men's straightforwardness and pragmatism. We might, but for now we don't... unless we work in the business world.

So please bear in mind that, as much as your partner loves you, he or she is not you: your partner does not think like you, and you two have different perspectives. Therefore, the more clues you give to each other about what truly matters to you, the better it is for your relationship. Men are distracted listeners, especially with women, so women taking the time to write down in a concise manner what they want is the best way to "spontaneously" induce the expected outcome. Also be aware, ladies! A burst of emotional talk shuts down men's ability to process: they go into emergency mode, and they will do what it takes to rapidly control your surge of emotions. Even if he has calmed you down, one way or the other, you won't have said what you needed to for him to understand: he does not want to do again what he thinks he did to trigger your frustration. The problem is that he does not really know what that is. Most likely he was not listening to what you were shouting at him, because he was thinking hard about the quickest way to calm you down.

Even if he adores you, he will not brainstorm over what might be the right move with you. He has no time nor energy for that because it is not his way to show you his love for you. If you want to limit your frustrations with your partner, you must be explicit, and in writing preferably, so he can return to it if need be. One of the things I ask women to do on my innovative website is to fill out a wish list of the things they would love their partner to do or get for them. I know it will not be an easy task to convince women to do this. However, I am positive that this is the only way to make sure that communication is crystal clear between both partners.

Misunderstandings are the primary challenge for a long-term relationship. We must do what it takes to learn to communicate in order to be heard and understood.

Part 3: The Power Of True Love

Life is so busy these days that we all tend to take what we have for granted.

Long-term couples face routine that is rarely glamorous; responsibilities, bank statements, and mortgage payments burden their reality. And they do not leave much time for fun. So, it is easy to associate our relationship with all the daily challenges we now have to face. It is also easy to blame our partner for what is wrong in our life. The reason we all look for a partner, besides the so-called biological need to have children, is because the true meaning of life is to be able to share it with someone. Being with someone should be a strong motivation to achieve more, to improve, and to move forward, and that makes life fulfilling. It is one thing to succeed professionally, and another thing to succeed financially. But very quickly the question comes: "Why am I doing all this?" The deep meaning of our career, of our life is to build a relationship that we can rely on, that we can plan for, and that we can rest on. It is the base of our personal life. It is the basis of our emotional fulfillment and balance.

As we grow older, life gets busier and busier, while our energy level does not increase. We need to proactively do things in order to maintain our energy level in the long run. Besides, life never fails to regularly knock us down in order to teach us lessons. Through them, we grow, and become better people. However, these life lessons usually take a toll on us. Whenever life sends us one of these challenges that leaves a mark, no one better than our partner can help us get through it better and help us stand up again. As our energy decreases our spirits are affected. During these critical moments in our life when we lose faith in our selves, and in our ability to overcome the difficulty, our partner's love and support keep us going, so that we eventually regain our self-confidence. No one knows you better than your long-term partner, not even your parents. Your parents know who you were as a child and an adolescent, but they don't truly know who you have become. Your life partner does. There's a saying that in difficult times you find out who your true friends are. Well, first and foremost, in difficult times, you know who your partner is; you know and feel the depth of the other's love and care.

Whenever two people in a relationship feel they should separate after spending decades together, I wish they would reflect back on what they went through together, on how each life event has made them a better, deeper person. I wish they would reflect on what role their partner played in that process. I am not saying that all separations are unjustified and should not happen. Very often, though, couples decide to separate for the wrong reasons. They follow the myth that elsewhere the grass is greener, when in fact all they need to do is take care of their own grass to make it greener.

Unfortunately, there is no immediate consequence to ignoring our relationship's needs. We all tend to overlook that essential part of our life. When our relationship dissolves though, in addition to the obvious financial consequences, the emotional distress is massive. This is one of the reasons so many people going through a divorce choose to hate each other rather than face the emotional void that will occur when they turn the page of this relationship in their life. The trend of individualism in our society gives us the illusion that we can be totally self-reliant: Women don't need men. Men don't need women. Moms don't need dads. Dads don't need moms. We don't need to socialize with neighbors, and so on. Even if we don't need to depend on one another, we do need to interact, and if we don't, we never become our better self.

In fact, being with others is what makes us expand and grow into better people. It is what makes us feel alive, and go beyond our own self. Of course we also need individual private time, but life is far richer if you have someone with whom you can share important moments in your life. Relationships are at the core of the human experience. Our romantic relationship is the primary relationship of our adult life, nothing less. A long-term relationship allows us to be truly our self and grow from there. During the day, at work, it is easy to have a mask and pretend to be someone else. But if we don't want to lose our self in that social masquerade, we'd better have someone at home who accepts the truth of who we are. We will be more likely, then, to able to get closer and closer to our life purpose. This is what leads to happiness.

The benefits go way beyond the cellular level of a family. If we learn to stay lovingly and respectfully in a relationship with someone different, we prepare the foundation of a true democracy, where no one overpowers the other. The collapse of the regular bonds forcing married people to stay together no matter what gives us the extraordinary opportunity to shape a truly respectful relationship, fulfilling for everyone. On a larger scale, isn't that the dream of all democracies? The task is challenging, though, because it takes energy, time, and work to succeed in a relationship on the basis that it could end tomorrow if we wanted it to. When faced with our first difficulty, whatever it is, we have the choice to work it out or not bother. It takes regular maintenance to experience mishaps without jeopardizing the whole relationship. This maintenance is called nurturing in the primary sense of the term. We need to feed the relationship so it is strong enough to go through storms and rough waters, and yet stay in shape. Nurturing a relationship is not necessarily easy, though, even if it is worth it.

Let's have a look at the three major ingredients that make nurturing your relationship possible. First, check on yourself. Be aware of what part you play in the dynamic. Decide that you will leave your comfort zone to improve this important part of your life. Second, learn to understand your partner. It is not an easy task to understand someone from the opposite gender. The best way to do that is to observe all your partner's reactions and try to put meaning to these reactions and to ask genuinely for confirmation, if need be. Third, learn to communicate efficiently. Your goal here is to ensure that the other can listen to what you are saying and understand what you mean. Very often it is like speaking another language. So the more you speak it, the easier it becomes. Little by little, year after year, you strengthen your relationship, and you deepen the understanding you have of the other, and more importantly of yourself. Eventually you know when to challenge, when to talk, when to support, and how to be efficient doing so. In short, you learn to love your partner. Then, the many years you have spent or will spend together become an asset. Your relationship is finally what it should be: the true haven everybody needs a relationship to be.

It would be a major mistake to write a book that aims to help long-term relationships without investigating today's parenting, and the impact it has on parents. The way we raise children today burdens our relationship with each other. In fact, the challenge today is to survive parenting. When children rule our lives and drain all our spare time and energy, what is left for our relationship?

4

PARENTING NEEDS TO EVOLVE

If you wonder why a book on long-term relationships would dedicate a full chapter to parenting, you probably don't have children. You are more than welcome, in that case, to skip this chapter. However, if you are considering having children, or if you already have any, what follows may be helpful.

While recent statistics show that a marriage without children is more likely to end in divorce, I have seen the loving bond between many parents completely crushed by the competing and overwhelming demands of their children. Staying in a relationship when love is long gone may be worse than a divorce. Parenting needs to be updated if we want relationships to thrive and children to be balanced. The space taken by children in our lives is really a cause for concern.

Between sleep deprivation and lack of time, it is easy to forget about the relationship that gave birth to the children. Parenting today faces unprecedented challenges that we should all reflect upon. In light of the ongoing pressure we all get from everywhere, it seems a good idea to focus on what truly matters.

Part 1: Parenting Today

Let's face the hard truth: aren't there times when you think your life would be so much easier without your children? When you and your partner look at each other in the evening with a fish-eyed gaze, exhausted from the daily battles with your children, can you picture how glamorous the evening could otherwise be? The truth is that today's parenting has never been more difficult. Against all political correctness, I will say that there are days when I wished I had made different choices. Although when I am honest, it is equally impossible to imagine my life without my children. Like most if not all parents, whatever the cost may be, I will do what it takes to lead them on the best possible track. However, I will never sacrifice my relationship with my husband because I know all too well the consequences for us and for the children.

When you have exhausted all the resources of your self-control each morning they must be ready for school, when you have asked the night before if the school bags were ready and an exasperated positive answer manages to reach you, and then everyone is delayed the next day because one child can't find his sweater, homework, or some other extremely important object, frustration leads the way. Blessed are we when both parents are on the same page most of the time. If not, the ensuing arguments can be endless. As soon as kids can talk, we as parents begin the endless process of negotiations, which we win at the beginning because we can outsmart little ones. Soon though, battles become fierce, and children quickly exhaust us because at 7 pm, the fifteenth "why?" just kills you. As a result, they win, too many times. We still have battles we are not ready to lose. All in all, as we age, we understand the years of life we lose in the process of having these arguments and we let more go. This is far from the idealistic vision of parenting in which the parent is always composed and each exchange is an opportunity for the child to grow in love. I personally hope that one day I will laugh about the hectic moments of my experience parenting. For now, though, I am deeply in the thick of it, and, like everyone else, I want to do my best.

Let's pause one second and focus on parenting techniques and child psychologist lecturers that inevitably make you feel bad about yourself. I won't name anyone. It is a bit too early to have identified enemies yet. Let me just tell you that one of the only parenting books that really taught me something I could use was a French doctoral thesis written in the 1980s on children's behavior starting at birth. This book's precisely described pattern of a child's daily behavior gave me a reference point for interpreting the needs of my first child for the first three years. The second book was handed to me by a neighbor in Hong Kong, after she had probably noticed that I was a complete wreck from sleep deprivation: my third child had gone through surgery at two months and when he was six months, he was still not sleeping through the night. I was on the verge of collapsing. The Contented Little Baby Book,[42] written by Gina Ford, was simply a blessing. Within five days of my reading the book, my baby slept through the night, and even now, he goes to bed very easily. The rest of the conferences I attended, books I read, and trainings I went

---

42 http://www.ezcouple.com/cbbbook

through did not help. On the contrary, they irritated me: at one conference in particular, when I realized that I had been lectured for two hours by a woman who had no children herself, her PhD did not do much in convincing me.

When it comes to parenting, theories are wonderful except that they rarely work. Every family has its own dynamic: we parent differently depending on where we live because the parenting pressure is different in different places. There are other variables that must be taken into account, such as birth order, personality, and, last, although not least, the parents' beliefs. As a result, there is not one answer, nor one technique that will suit everyone. When it is 7:38 am, and you have been calling each child for ten minutes to get in the car, knowing that leaving at 7:40 am makes everybody late – I am sorry, but compassion, mindfulness, and so forth are completely foreign at that particular moment. All parents know those moments.

The sense of entitlement our kids have in the western world makes our life seem impossible. In addition, this tendency is a slippery slope that leads to deep dissatisfaction sooner or later. Struggling is part of any learning process and sparing our children from struggling is a huge mistake. Reflection on our own childhood can be a good reminder of the value of struggling. I will always remember the French teacher I had in my first year of middle school and my junior year: I owe her everything I know in French. All students were scared of her; what she demanded from us was huge, and I remember many times when I thought that what she asked was impossible. It required a lot of work, time and energy, but it paid off later at college and at the university level. Although today I write mostly in English, whenever I write in French I am grateful: Mademoiselle Bessard gave me the tools to understand and appreciate the subtleties of my mother tongue.

Many things in life require the acquisition of knowledge before they become enjoyable. Take music for instance, a good twenty minutes a day of practice is required to start playing any instrument decently. Learning to read music is rarely fun, just like grammar in any language. Learning means integrating new concepts, and it challenges the comfort zone. Similarly to failure, struggle precedes the "a-ha" moments that make the learning process enjoyable. Failure teaches lessons like nothing else does. When parents submit to the dictatorship of their children they deprive them from learning resilience. They stop them from thinking through adversity. We will not change the equation that makes remembering what we learn the hard way much easier than what we learn the easy way. Struggling has never been fun. Even if the value of what we achieve is strongly related to the struggle we had to overcome, we rarely enjoy that phase. Those who have suffered very often transform their hardship into a valuable experience that makes their lives precious and meaningful. They have an understanding of a human heart that is far deeper than anyone who has not gone through the same traumas. I was struck by the depth of the words used by Father Boyle in Krista Tippet's interview on NPR[43] radio station, when he recalled what an ex-gang member said when he shared his story to the audience and the meaning he had found in it. The most effective people to really help at an emotional level those who are going through a specific trauma will be the ones who have gone through a similar trauma and survived it. They can relate to the suffering and help from their own experience by providing a paved road to overcome the trauma. No degree will ever replace that life experience. This is the extreme side of struggling and no child should ever come close to what I just described. Yet, the opposite extreme is definitely not the right road either. Overprotecting our children will not spare them from facing challenges that will cause

---

43 http://www.ezcouple.com/nprob3

them pain, sadness, and disappointment at some point in their lives: rather, we are depriving them from learning the best way to cope with and overcome challenges on their own. As adults, we all know how important this ability to transform a setback into a positive experience is, don't we? Yet it is an instinct for parents to spare their children as much as they can, forgetting the guiding role of the parent in the process.

By subscribing to a social pressure driven by fear and marketing, parents foster ailments and pathologies in their own children. A maddening schedule from an early age drives children to hyperactivity. I remember attending a conference in Hong Kong at which it was said that wandering time fosters creativity: after school activities should therefore be limited. We all remember these times in our childhood when we would look for shapes in the clouds and let our minds wander wherever our imagination would take them: often boredom would be the starting point. Check this article, "The Child Trap[44]" from the New Yorker, written by Joan Acocella in 2008, which is surprisingly accurate. For example, one problem today is that if you want your child to practice any sport you have no choice about how much time that demands: twice a week is the minimum required because competition is fierce and the possibility of a scholarship drives everybody nuts. This system might find the next Tiger Woods, or the next Kobe Bryant, but in the process it robs children, most of whom have no future in any sport, of the simple pleasure of participating in sports. Lucky are the children who very early on know that they love playing football or any other sport. The leisure to change your mind and try something else is for those who have not already been identified as talented. The talented ones are convinced that it is their sport, even if this conviction is only the result of pressure from the

---

44 http://www.ezcouple.com/nyer

adults around them.

Our anxiety over our children's future keeps them from experiencing and failing in order to learn more about themselves. Nobody wakes up one morning with a declared passion. Creativity does not come from sitting in an art class: it grows from dreams. A passion is revealed through a process that goes beyond the attraction of what is new. It may take years to find a true passion. Adult life makes trying things out difficult because our free time is limited. It is therefore important to let our children try and experience different things to give them a better understanding of who they are and what they will enjoy doing in the future. We all tend to project our own fears on our children, and our own view of success that most likely will be outdated by the time our children reach adulthood. My first son's kindergarten teacher in Singapore told me one thing that I will never forget: "Most likely," she said, "these kids will do jobs that don't even exist; our role is to teach them how to learn and stay curious." Indeed!

Regardless of the job we choose, we don't make it to the top without hard work and commitment. Determination and perseverance are critical to any success. It is the anti-quitting policy that leads to success. Real success is not the finish line of a race; it is an ongoing progression towards a moving goal. The drive that successful people have is an internal fuel that pushes them to go further and set new goals when the current one is achieved.

Contrary to the French educational system, which puts pressure on children to succeed academically from preschool, the American education system leaves little ones pressure-free, and gradually increases the pressure from first grade. My husband and I chose the latter for that reason, because we both believe that the French system crushes most of children's self-confidence. Of course, all educational systems have their flaws, usually the direct consequence of their advantages. The American system tells kids all day that they are great; the French system tells them all day that they are not good enough. American children start their adulthood life with an inflated sense of self-esteem, and then they are placed under the control of college professors. French children have little self-esteem; they place struggles on an altar to academic success that forbids them enjoying any success, but they are street-smart, inventive, and always ready to question authority and what is given to them. Too much or too little struggle is equally bad. Both systems would gain in incorporating some of the other's qualities. Often, we hear "kids are kids" to justify the unacceptable. Being a child is not an excuse for mediocre expectations. It gives children a false sense of success for which they will pay dearly sooner or later. Neither is being a child a waiver for misbehaving in public places or for being disrespectful. Children are a work in progress, and we, the parents, should provide the safe and loving environment for them to grow, experience, fail, and recover. This is the only time in one's life when failure does not cost much, when consequences are limited.

The good mother concept as understood here in the U.S. is deceptive, dangerous, and delusional. My understanding of the good mother concept is that it is tied to the amount of time and energy she dedicates to her children, with the idea that the more the better. This concept is flawed and unrealistic. The rule of "the more the better" that seems to define that concept is suffocating for children. On the one hand, it precludes the father from having a close and fulfilling relationship with his children. On the other hand, the omnipresent mother is a nightmare even for herself: she loses touch with her feminine side and fails to find her own passion in the process. Her children rule her life, and the only space left for the male partner is to be another child. The Berenstain Bears, to that extent, is a striking example of a mother-father relationship that would depress any newlyweds passionately in love with each other.

In <u>Bringing Up Bebe,</u>[45] P. Druckerman praises certain traits of French parenting, while Amy Chua in <u>Battle Hymn of the Tiger Mother</u>[46] condemns the easy going attitude of American parenting. I don't believe there is a miracle recipe for proper parenting, especially today with the role played by technology in our lives. I think the reason these two books received such frenzied media coverage is that they highlight two very important points overlooked by the usual maddening sources of parenting pressure:

Children's brain development keeps them from understanding the full scope of their actions until the age of about 20.

A mother is first a woman with her own life, desires and needs.

Parental guidance is therefore needed to instill morality and self-respect, and create habits that will serve children in the future. Take food as an example: no children will choose broccoli over French fries even if they are told that French fries might hurt them in the long run. That makes no sense to them because in their eyes the future is tomorrow, not in ten years. Parents have no choice but setting and sticking to rules if they want their children to eat healthfully while they grow. The problem with parents' fear of traumatizing children, and all the beautiful theories that use compassion and unconditional love in a deceptive way, is that limits are necessary for children to understand themselves. Being the one who sets the limits, with the light of the reality beyond the child in mind, is not a fun job, but it is one of the very important roles of a parent. A parent is a tutor; a tutor is not a flexible piece of wood that bends according to the sprout's desires.

45 http://www.ezcouple.com/bringup
46 http://www.ezcouple.com/tiger

Let me give you examples. When we moved into our current house, the previous owner had spent close to $5,000 in safety gear to protect her 15-month-old child. All the staircase banisters were protected, and every single drawer in the house and all the lower cabinets had safety locks that made opening them a nightmare. Rather than adjusting the house to the child, in France, we use playpens, adjusting the child to the house. A $90 playpen does a better job without making the whole family live a nightmare each time someone wanted to open a drawer. If you lose sight of your toddler, the child can get hurt despite the equipment; there is always something to climb on. In a playpen the child is safe; he may try to climb out, along the way creating neuro-pathways in his brain to find a way out. At some point, of course, he will, and his parents will watch him risk being unbalanced for a few seconds before his feet land on the other side. Then playpen time is over, and the child has learned a valuable lesson.

Another example comes from southeast Asia, where they wrap up newborn babies like sausages for the first two to three months. At first the idea made me feel claustrophobic, but when I watched my third child calm down and relax all wrapped up in his cotton towel, I understood the sense of safety induced by a containment mimicking the sensation he had in utero. A newborn is hypersensitive through every part of his body. Have you noticed how difficult it is to relax a newborn baby when you give him a bath? Being naked is stressful. Clothes and wrapping are both reassuring. Like bundling mimics being in utero, a playpen matches the early walker's dimensions; a full house does not.

Treating children like mini adults presumes that they have a mini adult brain. This is simply inaccurate. The brain is not fully formed before the age of 21; in fact the prefrontal cortex, referred to as the

<u>CEO of the brain, is not fully mature before then</u>.[47] As a result children go spontaneously to what will trigger immediate pleasure regardless of the consequences. And they are encouraged to do so through the fierce marketing of companies whose best interest is to target these wonderful customers. But we, the parents, know better; we want the best for our child in the long run. We know that children are driven by the desire for instant gratification, unaware of the consequences this strategy could lead to later on. Parents are acting upon the principle of delayed gratification when they nag their children with homework day after day: we all know that acceptance to a good college depends on academic performance. So from our child's preschool on, we look for the best school that will feed into the next best, and so on. When the child is four years old the road to Yale or Oxford is really long, yet we all dream of it. We visualize our child at twenty or thirty, having gone into a certain path; we perceive a potential here or there, and we push daily to guide our child into that lane. We do our best. This is the foundation of the daily battles we have with our children. This is the true nature of parenting: making sure we protect and prepare our children for what is to come, not knowing what it will be. In the midst of the overwhelming schedule we all have, we can forget what is truly important to teach our children.

Part 2: What We Should Teach Our Children

∽

Excelling in math and science may lead to a great college but it will never be enough to lead a great life. From an early age children should also be taught:

---

47 http://www.ezcouple.com/teenbr

1. Respect for and understanding of the other gender
2. Eating and sleeping habits that foster health
3. Respect for their parents and their mother in particular

Respect for and understanding of the other gender

The other gender is another planet for everyone. Yet, it can be a familiar planet if we travel there often, starting early on. Children exposed to different cultures have a better understanding of the world as it is: their own life and culture is viewed through the perspective of other lives and cultures. That fosters tolerance and respect, and it repels fear.

I think that many problems between men and women stem from ignorance and fear of the opposite gender. One of the things that strikes me here in California is how everything is gender-based, and how early kids are encouraged to interact only with their own gender. I do not understand why a co-ed school would not take the step to truly be co-educational: have boys and girls work together. Imagine if for all group projects, a boy was paired with a girl. Wouldn't that give each child a better understanding of the other gender, and more importantly respect for that gender? How can we expect children to have any peaceful interaction other than hormone-related ones when they only begin to interact with the other gender when their hormones kick in? In Hong Kong my son's fourth grade teacher had a very strong view on gender interaction that he disclosed on the first parents' night: "In my class," he said, "a boy will sit next to a girl at all times; and for every project a mixed pair will be assigned to the task. This is the only way for boys and girls to understand and respect each other. What is going on at recess does not matter. At the end of this year, each kid will have had the opportunity to understand the other gender a bit better." Often problems start to grow early in life, and the scope of the consequences is only perceived much later. Sexual assault and rape are the result of distorted perceptions and the inability or refusal to respect someone else.

Rape in college is a serious issue, and the staggering number of rapists who think that "no" means "yes," mostly unaware of the wrongdoing, reveals that somewhere along during their childhood education various lessons were missed. We need to start addressing issues of gender in kindergarten onwards. Not only do the statistics on rape in the US demonstrate in what regard women are held, they also betray a complete ignorance of how women communicate. If, before their hormonal surge, we taught children how to communicate efficiently with the other gender, we would provide space for cross-gender relationships that are nurturing and fulfilling for both. Otherwise we face what we have today: certain men viewing women as a piece of flesh to gratify their own sexual desire and an object that they can control. We can have laws against sexual harassment and against rape, but the root of the problem has to be addressed in childhood, in the neutral environment that school represents. I am shocked to see what kind of sexist insults my middle-schooler brings back from school. And he is in a private school that displays very strong values about the power of the words and minding other people's feelings. I can only imagine how much worse it can be elsewhere.

Repressing sexist language and behavior will not suffice. Complacency with boys' coercion of girls has to stop at home first. The strong disapproval of my husband and I, combined with immediate consequences, when we heard the name my son had called his sister during an argument should occur in every house. Women are not sex toys and those who think differently have to be taught otherwise.

A very large number of rapes in the U.S. are not reported because some survivors fear a second trauma in going through the proceedings that might get their rapist convicted. Most of them just want to forget the experience, as if a trauma like this could ever be forgotten, as if their crushed self-esteem will not hinder their life, as if their relationship with any male partner will not be critically affected in the future. For more on that matter please read the very well-documented article from Soraya Chemaly posted in October 2012 at the Huffington Post web site.[48] The severity of the consequences of rape for the survivor is not reflected in the social response, in part because this response depends on the legal definition of rape.

Data on rape, as a result, can be really misleading, especially when different countries are compared: For example, Sweden is said to be one of the western countries with the highest rate of rape. In Sweden, however, if a woman comes to the police to report the fact that her husband or her boyfriend has been raping her every day for the past few months, the police have to report each rape as a separate incident. Have a look at this article from the BBC's web site "Sweden's rape rate under the spotlight,"[49] written by Ruth Alexander, and you will get a better understanding of how difficult it is to analyze the data on rape in order to adjust a collective social response. Please note that there is close to no data regarding rape on men. In the U.S. in particular being the victim of rape is viewed as so unmanly that there is a collective mental block to addressing the issue of male rape: victims are buried in shame and many would rather die than report it, and that perpetuates a collective blind eye.

In the U.S. the official rate of rape does a poor job of reflecting reality, considering the number of unreported sexual assaults

---

48 http://www.ezcouple.com/huffpost102612
49 http://www.ezcouple.com/bbc0912

including rape[50]: the chances of a victim seeing her offender convicted are slim, and the reporting system as it is in colleges is shocking: the outcome and consequences of any sexual assault on a college campus depend on how the college staff, most likely insufficiently trained to cope and deal with the distressed declaration of a person victim of rape or other sexual assault, handles the report. Why are victims not well assisted or encouraged to go to federal court to get their rapist convicted? Rape is a crime. Would any homicide be kept within the college? Certainly not. Of course colleges want to address all rape and sexual assault on their campus in the best possible way; in reality the priority is preserving their connections and their reputation first. A college's reputation often prevails over the situation of student sexual assault. That student, however, needs a lot of support in order to go through the tedious process of legal report and what goes along. The unique character of each sexual assault rarely stands in front of the global reputation of a college. A strong policy against rape and rapists is yet to be in the best financial interest of colleges. That shows what little consideration these schools, and their communities as a whole, have for their female students, or for the human body in general. Boys are also raped in colleges. In fact, the US department of Education Office of Civil Rights reports in April 2011[51] that 6.1 percent of boys are victims of sexual assault or rape in college. The Office also gives specific guidelines[52] for schools, colleges and universities to comply with Title IX of the law against discrimination from 1972.

The data about rape and sexual assault in general may be difficult to interpret at times. However, it only reflects one side of the alarming problem. The data that apprehends rape and sexual assault through reporting, legal proceedings, and conviction, is necessarily limited.

50 http://www.ezcouple.com/rainn
51 http://www.ezcouple.com/whths
52 http://www.ezcouple.com/tix

Civil law or common law is based on the burden of proof: what you can't prove doesn't legally exist. Even if this might lead to distressing situations at times when a deserved conviction is nullified over an irregularity in the proceeding, this is the best protection of our individual rights. Unfortunately, it is often inadequate when rape is concerned: the scope of the trauma, the difficulty of providing material proof if the report is not made within 24 hours following the crime place prevention at the forefront of any collective strategies to reduce the incidence of rape.

It seems to me that any strategy should start with understanding our body and its sexual needs in the light of any interaction with someone else. The word sensuality is negatively connoted; the Merriam Webster dictionary even gives "debauchery" as a synonym. We are incarnated: our body drives our life as much as our brain does. It is delusional to ignore our senses and physical needs. Religions have tried in vain to banish the "sins" of the flesh, resulting in terrible transgressions: the Catholic Church pedophilia scandal is one example. No one can go against nature: physical contact between human beings is natural, though that does not mean everything is permitted. When children see their parents hugging or kissing, they understand what positive and consensual contact is. Repressing physical contact just exacerbates the need for physical contact. Linking moral value to abstinence is wrong. Questioning whether marital rape is a crime is also wrong. In California, in 2013, a law crafted in the 1870s stating that if the victim of the rape is not married, and the perpetrator was impersonating another man, the encounter is not rape, was used in appeal to overturn the conviction of Julio Morales[53] and his three-year prison sentence. This shows how little consideration society as a whole has for unmarried women. As of April 24, 2013, a bill changing

53 http://www.ezcouple.com/caltrial

that law has passed before the Senate on a reassuring 37-0 vote, and has been sent to the Assembly.

On a cellular level we need to leave the ground of protection to reach the ground of respect. Women in the West don't need protection: they need respect. It starts with self-respect: a girl who allows herself to be dead drunk and raped has no notion of self-respect. Regardless, the fact that she is drunk should not be considered extenuating circumstances for a rapist, because the lack of respect is total. And we may tolerate what we don't really know, but we can't fully respect it. Respect comes with education and awareness. It has to start with teaching our children how to respect their own body and everyone else's body.

Eating and sleeping habits that foster health

It seems pretty basic that one of the most important tasks with parenting is to teach children how to survive, in a strict sense. Yet our overindulging western countries have forgotten what it means: we must provide the body with what it needs to thrive: food, rest, and shelter in that order.

How many of us know how to cook from scratch? How many would be able to teach their children, from the immense variety of food and produce available, what to eat and when? In Asia, food is the base of traditional medicine. In every culture we used to know how to treat minor infections with something we ate or drank. Most of us have lost that critical knowledge, relying on medical pills or supplements to palliate our ignorance. We must learn and teach our children what foods are nutritious, what it means to have a balanced meal, and how to prepare a meal. This knowledge used to be transmitted by observation at home. I remember reading to my daughter a little book about apple pie that showed how the apples grow in the garden, how grandma would pick them, peel them, and cut them to prepare the apple pie, and how mommy now buys it from the store. The point is not whether or not we cook, it's that we don't know how to cook.

Think about the fact that there are over 7,500 varieties of apples in the world and over 2,500 just in the U.S.: how many do we know? For most people an apple is an apple. Similarly, there are at least 20 different types of green salad vegetables with various flavors. Have a look at the pictures on this French blog[54] to see how many you know, and like. You could add all sorts of kale and chard to your diet. The nutritional diversity of natural food is far superior to processed food, yet most of us would be clueless how to prepare most natural foods. I remember when I first arrived in Singapore how puzzled I was in front of vegetables I had never seen before. My mother, who came to visit me, would create associations by testing each, and she would tell me, for example, that this is a sort of cabbage: her cooking experience would find a way to accommodate them instantly. I would have been unable to do so without a tedious process of trial and error.

Nutrition should be taught to children very early: the problem is that today few adults truly know and are able to teach how to choose and eat fruits and vegetables. Even in the meat category, many of us don't go beyond chicken, turkey, lamb and beef, ignoring the diversity of game animals that are much leaner and in most cases more healthful. Although it may sound like science fiction to most people today, as a child I used to eat fowl, rabbit, pigeon, quail, goose, pheasant, boar, and probably others. We have a wealth of healthcare products in our food that we ignore. Eating is a blessing essential to our survival: isn't it a priority to teach that?

---

54 http://www.ezcouple.com/frblog

Taking care of the body's external hygiene is far more common. In fact in my children's school they even lecture in the 4th and 5th grades about puberty and what it looks and feels like. Amazingly, though, girls only get lectures about the female body and boys about the male body. Why don't we teach what the other gender's body looks like and feels as well? For those who have brothers and sisters, they might learn it at home but for the others? Don't you think that boys would benefit from learning about the female body cycle, and similarly girls would have a better understanding of their own difference by learning the subtle changes of the male body during puberty? I am told that we are lucky that the school provides these lectures. We probably are to some extent, but it is depressing to me to see that, there again, the gender wall is thick and high: the boys' lecture was done by a man and only fathers could be with them, and similarly for the girls the whole room was filled with only women.

When are we going to stop the hypocrisy of embarrassment when knowledge is critical to change the interaction between men and women? Would we rather see our preteens and teens view pornographic videos or pictures behind our backs to get an understanding of the other gender? Where do you think rapists who believe that "no" means "yes" get that idea? And we wonder why, in a world in which you can get a divorce almost overnight, relationships don't last! For centuries, men and women have met on a physical level because the latter had no choice: the binding commitment of marriage seasoned with religion made it compulsory for the wife to comply with her husband's desires. This is no longer true. Sex can no longer be determined solely from the perspective of the male, whether we like it or not.

Respect for their parents and their mother in particular

Teaching children about respect is critical to the balance of the family. It also teaches children how to behave with others. Respecting the parents does not mean creating fear. It means placing your romantic or married relationship first, and taking full charge of the leading role you, the parents, have. The stronger the relationship between the parents, the healthier the children will be. Being respected also implies resisting the insane parenting pressure that leads you to antidepressants and your child to the latest ADHD drug. Days are 24 hours long however you look at it, and it is delusional to stretch yourself in order to meet everybody's requirements. Between birthday parties, sports practice, and homework, there is enough to drive you insane. Often I hear that sports are good because they limit screen time, but escalating activities in order to control the invasion of technology in our life is a desperate way to handle that problem. It leaves no place for dreaming, and it ruins our schedule.

We end up being The Driver, at the children's expense. How can the parent be respected if this is the case? The child is so used to the fact that his parents constantly adjust to accommodate his demanding schedule that it encourages a sense of entitlement. The mother, who very often is the driver, housekeeper, etc., deserves no respect from the child's perspective. She does what she is supposed to do, like all the other moms. We are so spoiling our kids that we have no clue what to give them for their birthday or for Christmas, or we discover that what they want is outrageously expensive. Where is the respect for the work you do and the money you make? Where is the gratitude that fills the heart? We can't expect a mother who is treated like a servant all day long to be a charming partner at night.

Being respected is the first step in teaching respect. Saving some special time for your relationship is therefore a must. Taking time off from your children on a regular basis is the only way to keep these priorities straight. Each member of the family is a person but not everyone is equal. My teenager would certainly disagree with what I am about to say: Parents know more about life – they don't know it all, but they know more. They are in charge and that implies making decisions for those they must lead. Respect has to be mutual: we respect their feelings, and they respect our decisions even if they go against their feelings, because we know better. We might make stupid decisions along the way: they will survive. Nobody is perfect. We all need to adjust to the dynamics created by technology and globalization. Having a clear idea about who leads is stress-relieving for everyone. In addition, if your children respect you and your relationship with their other parent, they get precious information about themselves, on relationships in general, and on the intimate relationship they will have in the future with another human being.

Limiting your child's activities to what is manageable and healthy for him anchors him in reality, and helps him understand that life is about cycles. If there is one thing I believe is true about parenting, it's that clear limits are necessary for a child to grow with a strong sense of self because boundaries are the reference points by which he understands the world. Think of limits as a frame against which the child can bounce off until he is big enough to break the frame, like the aforementioned playpen. Children raised without limits in their family often look for those limits in the outer world, usually at their own expense. Drawing limits and boundaries often goes against the flow of a growing child, who is deeply self-centered and who constantly wants more. Yet that is the job of a responsible parent.

Parenting is about forgetting the urgency of the moment in order to be in tune with what will matter later. Thirty years from now this birthday party, this extra-curricular activity, this toy will have very little importance, if any. Is it therefore worth your sweat?

The western world is making the same mistake with parenting as it has done with medicine: compartmentalizing. The body is a bundle of organs and various cells orchestrated throughout by chemical reactions following an energy flow that we are only beginning to understand. This is far from the understanding of a compilation of organs organized by systems as taught in medical books. The human body is more complex, and treating one organ regardless of the rest of the body is bound to address only one side of the problem.

Similarly, a child's wellbeing can't be isolated from his parents' wellbeing. Parents' needs have to be taken into account in order to raise a balanced happy child. Most of the parenting techniques I have read about identify the child's priorities, and the parenting revolves around those. In theory it may not seem like a bad idea. In reality, however, it is delusional; a parent who is at his wits' end can no longer focus on his child's priorities because his own survival "fight or flight" instinct takes over. Any parent who is struggling with health, financial issues, or simply great fatigue has to focus on himself first, and rightly so. The child's wellbeing depends on the parent's wellbeing, and his or her ability to guide the child. We can endlessly debate what should or should not be done: regardless, the 24/7 job of being a parent can't be flawless. We all love our children dearly, and we want what is best for them. We all want to be the best parent we can be. We probably are, to some extent. More than anything else, what a child needs, besides the basic material things for his survival, is a happy healthy and balanced parent to look after him.

In fact every child needs two parents to make sure that one stays calm and balanced when the other loses it. Children love pushing their parents' buttons. It takes a true hero to stay calm when your buttons are pressed over and over. Unless you take medication that dulls your experience of negative events and emotions, I don't see how you can be a "good parent" one hundred percent of the time. In any case, is that really the goal? Being a good parent is not easy to define, given the number of factors that must be taken into consideration. We all do our best according to our own belief systems, and sometimes it is good enough and sometimes it is not. The truth is that raising a child is a unique experience that is challenging for all of us. We are all in search of help and advice when we enter parenthood, simply because it is overwhelming and deeply unsettling. We should never forget to nurture our relationship with our partner in the process. Here are a few points we would be better off remembering when we parent Junior:

1. First, we need to remember that Junior eventually chooses his own life. We can pray we will be proud of him, knowing that we will have no say in the critical choices he, who once was our baby, will make as an adult.

2. We must guide Junior, knowing that Junior learns mostly by watching us live. Take respect as an example: it is far more important that we respect our body, our rhythm, and our partner, than that we lecture Junior about respect.

3. We must protect Junior. In the western world, the main thing children need to be protected from is marketing. Businesses have found in children an amazing source of profit, and easily swayed demographic. Don't expect ethics to come into the picture: businesses are here to make money. So we, the parents, are the only shields our children have to protect them from the very professional marketing pressure. We need an awful lot of energy to do that because most of the time Junior doesn't want to be protected from it!

4. Last, we need to escape the pressure of parenting on a regular

basis to make sure we don't become exhausted. These days, parents are very often alone in raising their children. Never in human history have parents had so little support. Grandparents are far away, or they work, or they don't have the energy. Siblings are dealing with their own lives, and they are not necessarily close by, either. Community, afraid of "interfering", is not there to provide reliable help. Therefore, parents are on duty 24/7, 365 days a year. "No break parenting" is the fastest route for the couple to collapse, and ultimately for the family to go astray; love then becomes secondary as everybody is in survival mode. Finding help in order to have some time off should be a priority; your children will benefit from it as much as you will. They will have other experiences: the person who looks after them while you are away may teach them some skills you would not have. Your children will also learn to value your presence, they will respect your relationship, and they will become better husbands and wives in the future. Most importantly, they will learn that your world, the world, exists outside of their little person. They will learn that before being Mom and Dad, you are a woman and a man.

I will repeat it again and again: your relationship has to be your priority for everybody's sake!

Part 3: Technology And Parenting

If you think that this is unrelated to maintaining a relationship, you are somehow oblivious to the stress generated by this topic for a couple who has children. It is a primary concern that drains a lot of our energy, weighing on the relationship, causing undercurrents of tension and sometimes, open friction.

We adults are old enough and educated enough to discriminate the necessary from the unnecessary, the things that strengthen us from the ones that weaken us. We have the power and the intellect to resist marketing pressure. Theoretically. Our children don't. Children believe what they are told. Their emotions are on the surface, easily accessible. They are eager to learn, to have and to experience. They are like one big walking desire, ready to accept anything that looks appealing. All parents know that. The business world knows it, too, and uses that information as much as possible. Children, especially teenagers and late teenagers, are gold for marketing. With the invasion of technology in our lives, how do we deal with that? How do we protect our children from being eaten alive on the altar of marketing? I wish I had an answer. Ten years ago when the internet was not yet a major component of our lives, we could consider computers as dangerous things, and have children stay away from them. The truth is that, today, technology is far from being evil; it has transformed our ability to stay connected, to get information and much more. Who can live without the internet today? Who could live without a mobile phone?

Who would seriously consider today denying a child, who has a research project to do for school, the access to the internet? Who has the time to take that child to the library, search for an hour for information that may be outdated, when a Google search would have given up-to date information in minutes? Access to technology is the norm for our children. In fact they embrace it with eagerness... to play violent games more than anything else, to compromise their long-term reputation through social networking, and, occasionally, to study. Video games on the internet are appealing to younger and younger children, and we do not know the long-term consequences for these five and six-year-old kids who spend two to three hours a day absorbed in these games. The problem is that they have a growing brain, not a grown brain; they don't have yet a sense of self and others that would give them the necessary perspective to be discerning. When you combine good marketing and peer pressure you have a magic recipe... for businesses, not for children.

One of the daunting questions all parents have the minute a child is born is: What can I do to prepare my child for a future in which that child will thrive? Is giving into social pressure right, letting our children go with the flow in a river of temptations, some more detrimental than others? Is it right, really? My husband and I have had many debates over what (or how much) to let our kids do or have. We are fortunate enough to have lived in many very different places around the world, and that allows us to put any social or peer pressure in a global perspective. Yet, it is so hard to be one of the few who resist getting their kids an Xbox, for example; it is so hard to have a daily battle over screen time when homework has to be done in part on computers. Even if I throw myself daily into this daunting battle because I feel deep inside that raising kids with access to video games gives them a false sense of reality that they will pay for dearly later, I am not sure I am not fighting a losing battle. I am no match for the ever more enticing games that kids see at their friends' homes, on TV, and on the internet. I can't always be sitting next to them when they are at the computer to be sure they are not on the latest version of MineCraft instead of studying. Try to remember what it was like for you when you were sitting at your desk with a book from school opened in front of you. Try to recall a time when that lesson was really boring. Would you have resisted flipping the page if you could have had immediate access to the best game ever, to the latest message from your best friend? I was pretty conscientious, I still am, and yet, I know I would not have resisted.

Recently I listened to a <u>Ted Talk from a Swiss Professor named</u>

Dr Daphne Bavelier,[55] who has been conducting research on the effects of certain type of war games such as "Call of Duty" on the adult brain. My eldest son had great hopes that this would help his case for a coveted Xbox. In this Ted Talk video, Dr. Bavelier states that this particular type of war game increases the number of neuro-pathways and improves vision. This research has been conducted on adults playing for one hour a day. Even if this study opens the door to positive outcomes from playing video games, it does not say anything about the addictive nature of these games on children who play far more than an hour a day. It may improve their vision to some extent, but I doubt it will do anything for their social behavior and their understanding of human subtleties.

I still believe that video games featuring wars or terrorist types of environments have a detrimental influence on young brains. The values and ethics they convey are questionable, and the violence is omnipresent. As a result, violence and killing become casual. The realistic features of video games stir emotions linked to survival without truly preparing the body for survival. It is one thing to kill virtual people who can be resuscitated with some lines of computer code, it is another thing to end a life for real.

I am a big fan of the radio show On Being with Krista Tippett. I listened to her conversation with Maria Tatar,[56] a professor at Harvard University specializing in fairy tales, who says that current reality shows and TV series are based on fairy tale philosophies, aiming to give us clues about the world we live in. But I don't think she would include video games. In video games we are co-creator of the story, and emergency is at the root of all interactions. Furthermore, the war games do not reflect the trauma and fear felt by those who actually

---

55 http://www.ezcouple.com/vid7
56 http://www.ezcouple.com/nprob4

experience wars or terrorist attacks. In this time of overwhelming information with the world at our door via the internet, when we most need to reach a higher level of consciousness in order to discern the real from the fake, these games ground our kids in a level of survival whereby the other is an enemy or an ally. How does that help them understand and respect that which is different? How does that help us go beyond our fears with "a full moon in each/eye/ That is always saying/With that sweet moon/Language/What every other eye in/this world/Is dying to/Hear," as the poet Hafez beautifully says? Dr Bavelier says that her research aims to find what, in those games, really benefits the brain in order that other games, not violent war-type ones, can be created. Most likely, a video game featuring grabbing apples as they fall while preventing a tree from falling because of the wind, could create the same urgency that seems to develop reflexes in violent video games. Truth be told, do you think a gardening adventure will have the same success as a war game? I am skeptical. Hopefully I am wrong. Kids learn by doing and repeating what they see. How can any kind of violence be a good influence? We all know this answer, don't we? Businesses do, too. However, asking any business to limit its sales is basically asking a business to willingly die. It is delusional. What we can hope, though, is that the people behind the businesses have enough personal ethics to leave the easy road of quick profits that damage children, in either the short or long-term, for a more ethical road. Just like us, most of them have children, too.

Yet, however we may want CEOs and heads of marketing to behave, the truth is that we, the parents, control very little in regards to children's exposure to technology. Besides the computer that is big enough for us to see when a child is using it, consider the iPods, iPhones or other smartphones that all allow browsing and game play. Today if you give a child a simple phone that can only text it is perceived as a punishment. Children will never tell you that they want an iPod or an iPhone for the internet; the pitch will revolve around music, photos, and cool game apps. The next thing you know they have spent hours on YouTube watching series or who-knows what-without your knowing. My 14-year-old son and my soon-to-be 12-year-old daughter each have a phone. How do I know for sure whom they communicate with or what they watch? The truth is that I don't.

Some of you might think that children those ages don't need a phone. To be honest, I am the one that needs them to have a phone. When my eldest is invited to a Bar Mitzvah or other party, and my middle one goes to soccer practices in the evening, I love the fact that I can reach either of them in order to coordinate pick-ups. If anything happens, I know they can reach me. The only parents I know who don't give any phones to their kids when they can afford it are the ones who limit all social interactions to ones that happen with their supervision. Personally, it seems to me that the battle of a control freak is a lost battle. I don't think that refusing to allow them to attend the gatherings that make a teenager's social life is the best way to start the tricky teenage phase. Loosening control while staying in touch through phones is probably the safest way to approach that stage when a child will do whatever it takes to belong. Most importantly, we must keep the communication active: resisting a 12-year-old's desire for a phone is a wasted effort that might cost us dearly in our relationship with our child.

The world has changed so quickly and so drastically over the past century that I believe that all generations, one after the other, have been puzzled and perplexed by their teenager's needs and demands. Today we have no choice but to integrate the technology into our daily lives. This doesn't mean we don't have legitimate reasons to be worried: the world is far more dangerous than it has ever been for our children. Addictive substances are more readily available, hard to detect, and very cool. With access to technology, the dangerous world has passed through the front door of our homes and invaded every room in the house. We all know the terrible trauma caused by cyberbullying. The internet compounds the effect of any misdeed by irrevocably spreading the news. How do we protect our children from that? How do we make them understand that, whether they like it or not, what they write on the internet now will be available to everyone in the future.

I am not the only one concerned by these challenges. It does not take much research to find rising concerns about these risks for our kids. Check out this article from the Huffington Post "Zero to Eight: Children's Media Use in America,"[57] reporting on the data from a national survey[58] that was published in October 2011. In the meantime, though, marketing works at full speed. Facebook creates more and more games and services to hook our kids, intentionally closing its eyes to the fact that some of these kids are not old enough to be on Facebook. When a mom tells me that her child is not allowed to have a Facebook account, I am amazed by her confidence. It is so easy now for any child to have an account without their parent knowing about it. I don't believe that there is some magic recipe that could guide us through these challenges because they are unprecedented. We have no clue about the long-term consequences of too much screen time even if the screen is only two square inches. For now, I am praying that the structure we have given them since birth and the daily family dinner around a table when we all talk about our day will be enough to guide them through these fraught years.

That does not stop me, though, from talking to them about

57 http://www.ezcouple.com/huffpost201011
58 http://www.ezcouple.com/csm

what I learn about the effects of playing video games, <u>especially</u> <u>violent ones</u>[59], or the dangers of social networks, or even the risk of miscommunication through texting. My six-year-old listens to it all … looking forward to the time he will be allowed to have a phone or a tablet with a limited use time that he will already know how to bypass. There can't be any absolute limits on access to technology today, unless you live in a religious community that keeps technology at bay. We all need to review and upgrade constantly what we believe in, and adjust our behavior accordingly. Critical thinking and questioning are the only way to go. If we succeed in teaching our children from an early age that what they do has a huge impact on other people's lives, if we teach them that at the end of the day what matters is how they feel about what they have done that day, if we nurture the pride and the deep, loving emotion one feels when doing the right thing, then and only then, can technology be an asset.

In light of how little we control, transmitting our values is the best protection we can give our children.

---

59 http://www.ezcouple.com/nyt1213

5

UPDATING OUR COLLECTIVE BELIEFS

Part 1: Updating Our Beliefs About How We Live

⌒

We need to nurture our relationships like we need to exercise our body in order to make sure we keep our body in shape. Technology changes it all. Never before could we spend so much time on our own and yet never get bored. All we need is an internet connection. It is really stunning to realize how many relationships we can have today without ever meeting the person physically. Professionally, I only work with people I have never met in person. On a personal level, I contact most of my friends via phone, Skype, or social networks, and the actual physical time spent with them is minimal. I know I am no exception.

Before I develop further the reason we should learn self-control when it comes to technology, let me tell you what I do for a living. I run a few websites and for that purpose my work consists of finding information on the internet. My workday is spent in front of a computer; I read on iPad or Kindle, and on the go I use my iPhone extensively. I am an avid Skype user in order to keep in touch with my friends and family on the other side of the world. I order eighty percent of what I need online; I barely shop, and if it were not for shopping for the fresh produce that we eat religiously every day, I could do everything online.

Today, unless I consciously decide that I will spend physical time with someone, it may never happen. If I don't consciously dedicate some time to my husband and my children, we could all live next to each other but not with each other. Because I work with people in Asia, I could easily work around the clock, too, and follow my own schedule, regardless of the time. When researcher Dr. Daphne Bavelier states that the average video game user is 33-years-old, you realize how entertainment has become individualistic rather than social. People used to complain about television, saying that it stopped family conversations; at least, though, the whole family was watching the same thing. Now a family of five can easily be simultaneously watching their own movie on their own screen. And this is only the beginning. As everyone gets more in tune with their own interests, as free time is more and more limited, as the work day becomes less defined, the individualist trend in relaxation and entertainment will increase.

Yet, we are still human beings with a body that has its own rhythm and needs, with five senses given to us to fully perceive the world around us. It is delusional to fantasize about a world where we would not need to sleep, and we could be fed through pills or shakes, therefore reducing our need to urinate and defecate. The real human experience is utterly physical; it is the interactions and the exchange of feelings and sensations that make us feel alive and vibrant. We might consider eating and sleeping a waste of time; in fact throughout history men have searched for ways to reduce the need for food and sleep, mostly for purposes of war. Meanwhile, religions have more or less demonized the body and its needs in order to elevate the soul, as if the soul were not incarnated. Most religions advocate asceticism to achieve enlightened spirituality. In reality, connections are what lead us to a deeper spirituality, because it is through connections that we understand how that which is different matters.

It is our interactions with others that give us a sense of our own importance, and its relativity. Technology overstimulates sight and hearing, and our senses of smell, taste, and touch become secondary. Balance is what we should seek. All five senses can trigger immense pleasures, and the combination of all senses pleasantly stimulated at once create long-lasting memories of pure bliss. All of a sudden we resonate at a cellular level with what surrounds us, with an acute perception of what is outside of us. The anticipation of pleasure that the memory triggers at a sound, a smell, a caress, a flavor, or a vision is felt physically. This is why imagining is never enough, we need to live things to feel them.

Relationships based only on virtual communication will never reach the level of deep and true love, because physical contact and interaction is critical to access the whole being. Deep and true love happens when energies meet and mix, and when all our senses are positively stimulated in contact with that person. Many call that sharing, but "sharing" is now so overused that it is devoid of meaning. The depth and subtlety of the interactions between two people in love are not reflected in that term. This is so important to our understanding of ourselves as well as the understanding of others that we should not let technology deprive us of physical connections. We should be aware of the limitations of virtual connections when it comes to human experience.

Technology is a tool to serve us, real people. It gives us access to an unprecedented mass of information: this is fantastic. It opens so many doors to so many people. The drawback, though, is that an overwhelming abundance of information and stimulation can dictate a rhythm that is more draining than fulfilling. In other words, we should stay in control of our use of technology. Discernment should be the rule, because we live in marketing land and businesses have only one idea, making money from us. So, "addiction" and "craving" are two sweet words for the businesses that benefit from them. For us, however, whether food-related or not, the potential for dependence should make us vigilant. Addiction and cravings throw us out of balance and eventually destroy our lives.

Keeping in mind a clear sense of priorities is necessary today. No real relationship seems as pressing as an email notification, a chat message, or a phone call. The person who lives next to you day after day does not trigger the same adrenaline an online contact can trigger. Online relationships let the imagination work full speed when real relationships don't. Real relationships give us the opportunity to leave the public persona at the doorstep; and we can be truly ourselves, free of shame. Our schedule and our priorities are mostly left to us to decide, because everywhere, the pressure is so strong that no one can really cope with that pressure. We all create disappointment and deceptions as a result of that pressure, because our multitasking abilities are limited. We should just make sure we don't disappoint the ones who truly matter to us.

With our sedentary lives we all know that to stay healthy we need to move, and we are proactive in exercising. Similarly, nurturing a relationship has to be conscious because our lives do not leave space for proper spontaneous nurturing. A plant needs water every day to thrive. Try postponing the watering process until you have nothing else to do: the plant will have died long ago. There is no reason for your partner to still be in love with you twenty years from now if you don't do anything to fuel this love. So many parents forget about their relationship until their children are gone. What a mistake! There might still be respect left, but by then that is all. And most likely the two might separate, if they can afford a separation.

Understanding now that being proactive in nurturing our relationship is what will make it last. Making sure we schedule quality physical time with the ones we love, and our special partner in particular, should be a priority. If we don't do that consciously we might totally overlook it. There won't be any pressure to do the little things that matter to our partner. Only you can decide that these are the necessary steps to make your private life fulfilling. Think about the days you don't feel like exercising, and yet you do. You do so because you know it is good for you in the long run. We must all exercise the muscle of being with versus being next to. Technology will never teach us how to be with someone in a loving relationship or in a friendly relationship. We must practice to be good at it, because it is as important for our balance as exercising.

Part 2: Updating Our Beliefs About Men

Men's position of superiority in the western world has been seriously challenged over the last thirty years. As a result, men are stressed like never before. Most men now work harder to earn less; and their future is less predictable. Often men have to consider changing jobs or careers in order to make a living. Most of them lost a lot in the 2008 financial crisis. Many have needed to find a second career. In other words, their career is not linear anymore. Their sense of security has been deeply shaken. In addition to the massive economic instability we are going through, the internet is shaping our lives in such a way that many formerly high-paid employees have seen their income drop, while their individual work load increases. The world's competition comes to our homes through our computers. As Seth Godin, author and internet entrepreneur who founded Yoyodine and Squidoo, states in his interview with Brian Elliot dated February 7th 2013:[60] If your job is to perform a task, then you should be worried because there is someone somewhere in the world who will do that task more cheaply than you. Other jobs are no longer simply jobs: they are opportunities. In Godin's own terms, "Climbing the corporate ladder is a busted tradition." This is not necessarily a bad thing, but it implies massive adjustments in people's lives.

Men in particular have to take greater risks in order to succeed. Men with family are breadwinners to the core. They feel a huge responsibility to provide the financial support their family needs, even if their wife works. Most of their self-esteem is rooted in their professional life. So if they go through a tough time professionally, all of their energy will be spent trying to improve their situation. Little energy, often close to none, is left for the family. Needless to say, none is left for the couple. In addition, men are not only expected nowadays to help out at home, but they should also have an equal share in parenting. A long-term relationship is a partnership that should be a critical support during transition periods. A man who is challenged in his career will dedicate all his energy to finding another way to feel

---

60 http://www.ezcouple.com/vid8

good about himself. Usually that means working more, but it can also mean deluding himself about useless activities that he perceives as new opportunities.

When a man is challenged, he needs support that is not intrusive. A man is not a child, and he should not be treated as such. Many women wrongly choose the road of mothering their partner: it might bring temporary relief to the man, but in the long run, it jeopardizes his self-esteem. Is the Ultimate Guy to be mothered? In reality, simply being there can be enough. It is not time that he can give much of, anyway; he does not need much, either. His home more than ever needs to be a peaceful place.

Neither does that mean that the woman in the relationship should feel miserable and keep it to herself, accepting a form of selfish behavior from her partner without a word of protest. This is a time where her focus should primarily be on herself and on the rest of the family. This is the only way to maintain a loving atmosphere that will feed everyone in the household, including her partner. Eventually he will settle into a new order that might please him more than he suspects. The submissive woman is a dying concept that belongs in the past. The all-too-powerful man in a relationship is also a dying concept. Men need to adjust their sense of self as a man at many levels, and their wife can be a tremendous help in making the transition as smooth as possible. A long-term relationship makes it easier to go through hardship.

It also seems that the warrior man, tough at all times, and, let's face it, pretty uncomplicated, is a dying concept. If you look at the transposition of warrior behavior and achievement in the economic field, many successful men have little to do with this concept of the uncompromising, heartless authority figure. Check the Forbes ranking of the billionaires below forty[61]: the most successful in the ranking are internet entrepreneurs who impress with their ideas and determination rather than by what they control. Their demeanor reflects a new trend. The successful guy is very often an IT guy who is far from looking like the ideal strong, model male portrayed in our subconscious minds. Money, real money, belongs to these 25 to 35-something men who seem to have ideals closer to the feminine side. They don't seem to mind vulnerability the way most traditional men of an older generation would. They are beyond that. When you take a close look at most of the top success stories of the internet, you see male figures different from the usual boastful, successful guy. These new success stories lead the way in a new way of being masculine. Most likely without realizing it, they have grasped the concept of vulnerability as defined by Brene Brown Phd, American scholar, author, and public speaker, who is currently a research professor at the University of Houston Graduate College of Social Work. Brown is famous for conducting years of research during which she discovered the wealth of opportunities in being vulnerable.

These new men have understood that within vulnerability lie flexibility and creativity. Until recently, being vulnerable was not really valued, especially for men. We have associated vulnerability with the need for protection. This is probably why women are more familiar with the concept, having been taught for centuries that they need to be protected. They have never been pressured to be tough and strong, and never cry. In fact the opposite is associated with stereotyped femininity. What is fascinating is that our ideas about vulnerability are starting to change: the idea of vulnerability has become worth investigating. In her Ted Talk, The Power of Vulnerability[62], Brene

---

61 http://www.ezcouple.com/forbes
62 http://www.ezcouple.com/vid9

Brown argues that suppressing a feeling does not make it disappear. I also recommend that you listen to her interview with Krista Tippett[63] on the "On Being" NPR show. Her Ted Talk has been a tremendous success because shutting down and pretending that everything is fine when it is not no longer works. As uncomfortable as feeling vulnerable may be, she explains how it is the only path to fulfillment. Suppressing feelings never makes them disappear; they simply harm the body. Suppressing a feeling simply creates a blockage that, sooner or later, leads to physical ailments. In fact so many illnesses, if not all illnesses, result from unresolved traumas or emotional blockages. Please read Biology of Belief, by Bruce Lipton[64], to learn more about the chemical reactions caused by emotions. We women know that it makes no sense to ignore overwhelming feelings of fear, distress, shame, or sadness. However, for a lot of men, shame stops them from acknowledging, especially in front of their wife, the struggle they are facing. This doesn't mean the modern man is a "girl"; he is not going to be crying all day, either. He is sensitive, and he uses this sensitivity to better understand his actions. This man uses his brain and heart much more than his other muscles. The outstanding success of these young IT guys shows that not only it is okay to be vulnerable, but it may also be the direct way to success. This idea opens a completely new perspective on being a successful male figure. It also translates to the intimacy of men's long-term relationships: being okay with being vulnerable relieves the pressure that a lot of men still feel trying to achieve an outdated ideal. It opens the possibility of a constructive dialogue with the female partner, based on respect.

---

63 http://www.ezcouple.com/nprob5
64 http://www.ezcouple.com/bbelief

Part 3: Updating Our Beliefs About Women

A serious update is needed for our concept of romance in our daily lives, if we don't want it to become obsolete. Many women claim that men stop being romantic after they have been in a relationship for some time. They would love their male partner to be more romantic, they would love him to show his love with flowers, romantic outings, and his full attention. And, of course, they expect him to do all these things spontaneously, just like he did when the relationship started. This concept for romance has been distorted. The first definition given by the Merriam Webster dictionary is "a (1): a medieval tale based on legend, chivalric love and adventure, or the supernatural (2): a prose narrative treating imaginary characters involved in events remote in time or place and usually heroic, adventurous, or mysterious (3): a love story especially in the form of a novel." What these three sub-definitions have in common is the fake or artificial character of romance, suggesting the strong role of the imagination.

The origin of the term "romance" goes back to the fourteenth century when a man could not touch a woman who did not belong to him. Courtship during the time of chivalry was about finding ways to express love and desire via artifacts because all physical contact was strictly forbidden outside a formal and official relationship. In this male-female interaction, the man initiates all the moves and action while the woman waits and receives. A woman then was highly dependent on men: her freedom of speech and action were restricted.

Courtship throughout the centuries has kept the nature of the chivalric, evolving only in the type of artifacts used. Women today tend to mix up romantic behavior and courtship behavior. They are, in fact, different, because they come at different times in the relationship.

Some men can be romantic beyond the courtship, but it will take some effort on their part. Women need romantic behavior from their male partner because it makes them feel special. However, this need to feel like a special, precious person could be addressed without using romantic behavior that is a throwback to the past centuries.

In 2013 a woman can be emotionally independent and self-reliant. Women nowadays are entitled to a grown-up love in which they are proactive. Romance dictates the behavior and actions of a man towards the woman that he loves in order to possess her. Do women still want to be possessed, or do they want to be loved and respected? I deeply believe that if women had not been immersed in fairy tales from an early age, they would not be so demanding with their male partner. These fairy tales, distorted by Disney (I am sure Maria Tatar would disapprove of me saying that because she strongly believes that there is no original version of a fairy tale), originally taught lessons about the feminine and masculine side within one person. This is one of the true value of these tales: they help solve psychological dilemma over feminine and masculine qualities by providing a way to combine them harmoniously. Disney has whitewashed their symbolism confining both genders to very static roles.

The stories as Disney presents them lead little girls to believe that Prince Charming, a highly romantic, almost psychic male figure is the norm. Nobody bothers to notice that all the famous fairy tales end with the wedding, with a wonderful sentence such as "they lived happily ever after." The ending at the wedding implies that courtship is the rule of behavior for the couple and the recipe for happiness in the long run; no wonder so many couples don't make it over time! Kindness, caring, and deep love are not romance. That kind of romance is an artifact from a time when women's very existence depended on how they were viewed, first by their father, then by their husband. Isn't it about time we drop that artifact as a definition of love? Flowers can be nice, but a man who helps his wife when both are tired at night, or a man who makes sure that his wife will have some pleasant time for herself on a regular basis, that man is showing his love in a very meaningful way.

Expecting traditional romance in the long run puts enormous pressure on men to comply with a one-size-fits-all protocol in their interaction with their wife, that they have less and less time and energy to cope with. In addition, it is deeply unfair: the whole purpose of courtship was to possess a woman. Men are not programmed to care about obviously expressing their love a certain way past the seduction stage. It is a huge effort for them to remember to be romantic; it is rarely spontaneous. Does that mean that they are unable to love a woman once they have sealed the deal? No, of course not! Men are amazing lovers who go well beyond sex to show their love and care for a woman. But they will do it their own way without thinking further. It is simplistic to think that most women are as tacky as Barbie dolls, and that most men think only about sex. Women do like flowers, beautiful settings, sweet words, and so on. Men do like sex much more than most women. That does not define the sexes, though.

We would all gain from searching into the depth of the other gender. We would definitely learn a lot. While immersing myself as much as possible into men's minds to create EZcouple.com, it was striking to me to see how much I learnt. Men are straightforward, efficient in many ways, and action driven. I became a better person in learning to apply their pragmatism. Men and women are different and each perspective complements the other. Romance, the way it is understood today, ridicules men as well as women, without addressing the needs of either. The only reason men seem to suffer less in most relationships is that they are used to relying emotionally on themselves first. They have thousands of years of experience relying on themselves, while we women only have a little over 40 years. Throughout time, most women have been raised to exist through a male. For a long time, their value and self-worth depended only on their capacity to be successful in the domestic field (marriage and children). Even today this idea remains in the collective beliefs system of most western democracies. When you think about it, since when it is fine for a woman to be single, independent financially, and happy? It seems to me that that is very new, and that there is still a lot of resistance to that idea. I have come to believe that fulfillment for a woman comes from feeling special, while men need to feel powerful. I also believe that fulfillment is an intimate, very personal road, and it should not be sought through someone else.

Women should start being happy with themselves first, before searching for happiness elsewhere. Being needy in a relationship is a recipe for disaster. We women have little experience of true independence, and we are still learning. The best route to a balanced relationship is for no one to be draining the other's energy. A dependent, submissive woman fuels a relationship based on power. Inevitably, every aspect of the relationship becomes twisted: control rules the relationship. On the other hand, an emotionally self-reliant woman sets respect as the core value of her relationship. Respect is the foundation for a deep love. Romance and the artifacts that come along with it then become a bonus, not a prerequisite. Nobody is taken for granted in a relationship in which respect is the leading value. The simplistic interaction between a man and a woman we have known for centuries cannot last when we all have the opportunity to choose a different partner if and when we wish to. Considering what we have on our plate every day, our relationship has to be worth working at. Building her self-esteem on her own first should be the priority for any woman. The modern woman is proactive with her life: she is still caring, but she follows her own values and her internal compass. She is a far more interesting partner than the submissive wife.

Part 4: Updating Our Beliefs About Sex

Loving sexual intercourse has everything to do with vulnerability. When we go beyond the passionate stage where a simple look or caress would suffice to ignite sexual desire, sexual intercourse becomes a new adventure. It can evolve into the culmination of a deep, loving relationship. Or, it can become a chore for one, and a hygienic move for the other. My research on sex here in the U.S. has stunned me. I heard and read about deals made around sex and oral sex, about women lingering in the kitchen at night because they dread the encounter in the bedroom, and about the acceptable number of times per week of sexual intercourses. Are we machines? Do we realize how degrading both for men and women this vision of sex can be? Is that what love is about? I read everywhere that men need sex; let me add that women do, too. We have many other basic needs such as eating and sleeping that we don't throw in other people's face as an excuse to abuse them. We successfully manage to fulfill basic survival needs by injecting some emotions and intelligence in the process. As a result these needs leave the physical plane to become an experience and an event, acknowledged and respected by all.

Sex on the other hand, still belongs to the secretive side of a relationship, rarely debated publicly. As a result many misconceptions come from the abundant and mostly inaccurate information one can find online, depicting sex as an exercise at best and as a perversion at worst. Usually the information on the subject barely goes beyond the physical, and sex is treated like nothing more than exercise. Hence, performance and other concepts belonging to sports are the focus whenever sex is talked about. Yet, this focus entirely misses the point and the importance of sex in human lives.

Sex is the opportunity for a unique connection with another human being. It is the ultimate of physical exchange and emotions all at the same time. It is the deepest physical connection with oneself as well. The intensity of what goes on during sexual intercourse has nothing to do with any sport of any kind. Keeping sex at a pure physical level takes humans back to animality. If we leave the animal kingdom, where sex is only associated with reproduction, we can start considering sexual intercourse in a light other than our need for it. Men in particular have other ways besides sex to relax; please check the next chapter for more details about that.

When the need for sex is combined with the will to give, to open our self to the other, the relationship reaches a deeper level. Acknowledging a need without overpowering anybody while addressing it is being vulnerable. We all are vulnerable, to some extent. Being vulnerable is inherent to being mortal: being alive will end one day. This realization puts everything in perspective by highlighting the relativity of our own existence. Failing is part of being human. In fact failures offer many opportunities to learn and improve. Being vulnerable is accepting the risk of failure. In the discomfort of vulnerability, we open up to new opportunities. Many couples have a very boring sex life because they never introduce vulnerability into this interaction, so they never dare doing anything different. Life in general is about being curious and exploring. Applied to sex, being curious and willing to explore means getting to know one's partner in a way that enriches one's own experience. In the process we get to know ourselves better.

Long-term relationships give us the opportunity to make sex a journey to unknown dimensions of our selves in our daily lives. The trust that should result from the years spent together can help us overcome deep traumas that could otherwise totally prevent our ability to relax in sexual intercourse. So many people have been abused sexually in their childhood; so many people have never addressed that issue, even though the impact on their life is huge. If we put vulnerability at the heart of our relationship's sexuality, we can be open, be helped, and heal. In addition to the physical pleasure of sex, we create deep and beautiful emotions with our partner that only a couple can ever share. We marry, in the most beautiful way, our mind, heart, and body for a combined emotional and physical experience.

In other words, fulfilling sexual intercourse has to go beyond satisfying a need for it in order to become truly pleasurable. It seems rather obvious when it comes to eating: we are particular and choosy about finding something palatable to relieve our hunger. Similarly, we should be particular, demanding, and selective when we feel the need for sex. That kind of discrimination never goes well with a systemic approach or a rigorous schedule. In fact satisfying our need for sex is far more difficult than relieving thirst or hunger because it involves another individual. So, besides the need for sex, caring for the other has to kick in as well. Isn't that what a civilized attitude should be? Taking care of our own needs without abusing anyone; compromising if necessary to make sure the other can live and thrive. Isn't it about time some civilization is brought into the intimate life of a couple?

Having regular sexual intercourse based on mutual respect and deep love of the other is what really distinguishes human beings from all other animals on this earth. So put aside the rules you read or hear; put aside the stupid social pressure based on dubious data about how many times the average couple has sex. Do you seriously believe that people would speak honestly about that to a complete stranger? Your sexuality is your own. Nobody needs to know about it. If you ever face a difficulty on that level in your relationship, take it as an opportunity to grow and find out more about yourself. At no point should sex be an obligation. Consensual sex has many benefits[65] that should not be understated, but sex is only one aspect of a relationship. It is the icing on the cake but not the cake itself. Just as you need the cake to put the icing on top, you need a loving relationship to have a fulfilling sex life. The time when marriage presumed regular sexual intercourse, usually according to the man's desires, belongs in the past. For the better.

Feeling vulnerable is inherent to being human. Exploring vulnerability is probably the best way to access a deeper understanding of the other. Vulnerability opens the door to meaningful sex. We are far from "Cougar Town"-type TV shows in which sex cards are given to the husband as a reward for him being nice. Beyond a mutually agreed-upon physical interaction, sex becomes the opportunity for a deeper understanding of the partner.

To me, sex used as a reward – and withholding sex as a punishment – is simply horrendous. Reducing sex to a game or a deal brings it down to the level of pornography and prostitution. In pornography and prostitution, women are utilized, like tools. In a long-term relationship where love and respect are paramount, sex should be the ultimate connection between two people who agree to expose themselves, physically and emotionally, to the other. It is about mutually giving and receiving in an intense interaction. In fact we are exposing much more than our body in that moment, whether we are aware of it or not. Sex should be a special communion cherished by both partners.

Sex, as a stress reliever for men, as a justification for a woman submitting to a rhythm that does not feel right for her, is just degrading

---

65 http://www.ezcouple.com/huffpost080212

women. It confirms the idea that women have been created for men's pleasure… and downfall, if we believe the Adam and Eve story. This is an outdated vision of the world. Although the concept seems to take time to sink in for some people, a woman is not a sheep to be sacrificed on the altar of her husband's need for sex. That is not what respect is about.

The reality today is that sex is no longer a prerequisite for a relationship to last; it is a bonus. Men who want more should create the right circumstances for more. Unless they explore and face their own vulnerability, they are doomed to fail because they will not understand what it takes to create the proper environment for a woman to be in the mood for sex.

A woman is not a sex toy and she never should be, unless what she wants is to be with a guy who is nothing more than a wallet. Toys and wallets are both objects, not people. Vulnerability is in a sphere they don't have access to. So is happiness.

6

WHAT WOMEN NEED TO CHANGE

Part 1: Drop The Myth Of The Perfect Mom

Children's books give typical examples of perfect mothers and we tend to forget how fictional they are at every level. For those of you who don't know Mother Bear, she is the ultimate mom. She is the mother in the Berenstain Bears family. In our family we absolutely love the Berenstain Bears family in their big tree house down a sunny dirt road in Bear Country. They have an answer for almost every problem any family encounters with parenting until children reach the age of eight or nine years old. Mother Bear is the kind of mother I wish I could be, but know that I never will be. She is always composed, always patient, and always available. Even when she is about to lose it, during Chores[66] for example, she does not; and she welcomes Papa Bear's ideas even if cleaning up is not his skill, nor, in Bear Country, his duty! Well, the truth is, we love these books because they convey good values in a simple fashion that we find harder and harder to do.

At the same time, however, I can't help being irritated; but not half as much as I was with Olivia's mom, who, on demand, MAKES a soccer shirt to Olivia's liking. Come on! Is there any mother out there who does that? Doesn't she have anything else to do? Well, Olivia's mom is the mother you wish you had, but she is not the mother you can be unless you live in the middle of the countryside with no internet connection, no TV, and your first neighbor is 50 miles away. So, we stopped reading Olivia fairly soon, not only because it was triggering my own insecurity as a mother, but also because my children very quickly lost all interest in this series. Mother Bear is much more effective than Olivia's mother in having me question my mothering abilities because she is credible...to an extent. Mother Bear is challenged by Brother Bear and Sister Bear the way we, moms, are challenged.

And it is fascinating to me to see how she responds when I would simply yell at my children to stop. Take The Berenstain Bears Get The Gimmies[67] for instance. She finishes getting her groceries and paying for them with screaming children around her. She is annoyed, but she does not make a peep: she just puts up with it and waits until she can think about a solution for later. I don't know if it has anything to do with the fact that I have been travelling with my children since their birth, so many times on long flights, suffering from jet lag, but I have

---

66 http://www.ezcouple.com/chores
67 http://www.ezcouple.com/gimmies

never tolerated any screaming in public places. I have always had an acute sense that others should not be subjected to my challenges as parent. They probably have their own challenges and they deserve to have a peaceful flight, especially when it is a 12 or 13-hour flight. The saying "kids are kids" has never been an excuse in our family. If kids can't behave in public, then keep them home! For us it was not an option to put up with screaming kids, considering how far we live from France and how often we travel there. My children had to behave. And they did, and they still behave in public, even if they often catch up at home! I learned very quickly how to make sure a baby, even a newborn, stays calm throughout a long trip. Feeding him at take-off and again on landing relieves all pain resulting from ear pressure that would make a baby cry.

Mother Bear's goal is to always teach a lesson without traumatizing her children. Don't we all love that? The problem is, at least for me, that I do not have the time or the energy to do that 12 to 14 hours a day, for three kids. You may think that I am exaggerating. Kids don't always misbehave, so the 14-hour period is unfair, and when they are in school, it drops to eight hours. First, while it is true that they don't always misbehave, when you have three, there is always one who needs your attention or intervention. Second, don't forget that there is a really long period before they are old enough to go to school, and then, morning hours and evening hours count double. For example, last night we read Baby Makes Five. If viewing a video of #2 when he was a baby was enough to tackle the anxiety of #2 when #3 arrives, there would not be zillions of books on the subject of sibling rivalry, don't you think? In a sense the Berenstain Bears make me feel better because I am sure I would be a much better mother in a much simpler world. The Bear family down the sunny dirt road do not even have to wear any shoes!

My only big problem with the Berenstain Bears is that the couple, Papa and Mama, has no existence outside parenting their cubs. Children's books are based on children's perspective. But isn't it about time for children's books to teach kids that there is a life outside of them? Most children's books have an outdated view on couples and parenting. They are based on the assumption that once the couple is formed, all the attention should be placed on the children. That may have worked in the '50s, but, now, presuming a relationship will last without proactive intervention is a dangerous assumption. Showing children an archaic view of a couple who are nothing but parents in book after book is distorting the truth. And soon they are introduced to books that present loving pictures of a couple divorcing, and then books showing how wonderful it is to have step sisters, brothers, two houses and so on.

Couldn't we update these books so they teach kids that their parents are individual beings with needs, too? When I look at Mother Bear and Papa Bear, I really wonder what kind of love life they have. Mother Bear is not the ultimate sexy wife, and Papa Bear is not Prince Charming. We are in a bear world after all, so the authors probably stick to animal kingdom rules where sex is only linked to reproduction. Since they are mimicking human lives though, we could expect a bit of a spark, between the two. Even if sex is a private thing that should remain private from everyone including the children, sex brings intimacy that shows outside the bedroom. Seeing their parents loving one another has never hurt any children. On the contrary, not only is it the best way to teach them how to love someone else, but it also gives them this secure bond they can grow from. Berenstains advocates will argue that Mother Bear and Papa Bear care for one another. Indeed they do. All the good parts of romance however are long gone. Papa Bear acts like a child most of the time, and Mother Bear perpetuates the outdated concept that only the mom knows what is best.

We all are beings of desire who want to seduce and be seduced. A relationship with no seduction becomes a slippery slope for both partners. This is not new. What is fairly new is that women do not have to stay in a relationship if they don't feel loved and praised anymore. This is also true for men. Women, just like men, need more than to be cared for. In today's world, we should never take anything for granted. Relationships go through cycles, and we need to nurture our relationship if we want it to last. There is no such thing as a perfect mother. It is unrealistic to aim for that.

Women have a genetic ability to understand cycles and respect them. The fact that they have begun to have a more prominent role in the outer world is a blessing, even if it seems to unsettle the foundations of our society.

Part 2: Embrace Women's Understanding Of Cycles

Some men may feel threatened by the increasing numbers of women in the business and political world. Although understandable, I believe it is an opportunity for everyone, men included. Most problems we currently face as modern nations are linked to the fact that we have lost our connection with rhythms and cycles. It is not that these rhythms and cycles have disappeared; in fact they are the only steady and predictable occurrences in our world today. We have, however, been ignoring them. So, instead of working with them, they are imposed on us and we are not prepared. Working with them would mean accepting and respecting these cycles, preparing for the downturn when we are in the upturn. Women have an extraordinary ability to stay in tune with the concept of cycle.

The very first cycle is, of course, the female body's monthly preparation for procreation. As annoying as monthly periods may be, they act as a reminder that we belong to something much bigger than ourselves, over which we have no control. The medical world has tried to control that monthly reminder, treating it as a burden when it is actually a fantastic detoxifying process. Birth control pills are used to control, regulate, and shorten this monthly release. These pills have numerous side effects: one that may be less obvious is that it distorts the messages sent by the female body through the monthly periods. The barometer of internal balance that natural periods represent is switched off. When a woman is taking the Pill, she can mark the calendar knowing precisely the day the next period will come. If she's not taking the Pill, a woman has to be more in tune with her body, watching closely for the signs that will announce the end of one cycle and the beginning of the next. She therefore develops a deep understanding of subtle signs. First, she recognizes them more easily and then, as time passes she is able to give meaning to them. Life is nothing but a succession of subtle signs paving the way for outcomes long before these outcomes are obvious.

The world in which we live in has lost all respect for seasons, and for human cycles. As a result, kids have become mini adults, and weekly breaks from all activity to reconnect with oneself and the divine are not respected. "Divine" here should not be taken in a religious way. Divine represents what is beyond us, what is bigger than we are, so it could easily represent a religious belief, and it should also speak to non-believers as meaning the universal interconnection between all. What seems "beyond" us right now is a fact, not a belief. The moon's cycle, earth's rotation; these are facts. We would all gain greatly by reconnecting with these cycles that govern our lives whether we like them or not.

Women have the ability to do that; they have a long-term view, a capacity to anticipate and see something coming way before material signs show. The more we trust this feminine intuition, the better the world will be. Women are not power-seekers per se; they are interested in goals beyond immediate gratifications. And most importantly, most of us are ethical because we have been brought up to care; working for the greater good is attractive and meaningful to us. In our daily lives, we must have a deep understanding of the whole picture to juggle work, household, kids, groceries, and so forth. The wide range of the tasks we tackle on a daily basis would benefit greatly to the world. This ability, combined with the sharpness, pragmatism, efficiency, and action-driven characterizing masculine traits, can do miracles.

The Chinese understood that long ago: balance comes from the right combination of Yin (ultimate feminine) and Yang (ultimate masculine). This is why we should take a closer look at our relationship. Our relationship is, at the family level, the representation of this yin-yang balance at play. Balancing these two traits will provide important clues on how to manage male-female interaction in the workplace on a much larger scale. It is about time we all go beyond the prejudiced ideas we have about the other gender, and start focusing on each gender's assets. Women are plagued by insecurity, which passed from generation to generation.

Few of us have the self-confidence that would allow us to blossom and express our potential. Even at the workplace women pretend to be self-confident by adopting a male attitude, like putting on a hat in the morning. Women's self-confidence is deeply rooted in the psyche: external acknowledgment matters, but it must also feel right. Men's self-confidence on the other hand is directly related to the outcome of their actions: as a result, clearly identified successes, such as making more money or getting a reward build their self-confidence. For women this is not enough. The outcome of their actions must resonate with how they feel. How they feel is partly in tune with some universal knowledge that is beyond us all. This connection to whether a position feels right or not regardless of other factors is a formidable asset: it is like an eye that could see beyond what is visible. Therein lies the amazing potential of women to lead in the business world. Imagine if all the high officials in Washington, following Hillary Clinton's example, decided to work from 8am to 7pm. If all the leaders set an example by having a proper lunch break, do you seriously think it would hurt the economy? I am not Hillary Clinton and I have not had the privilege of meeting her, so I can't know if there was any reason other than caring for her staff that made her model a reasonable work day for them. Maybe she also knows that a person who has a personal life is more balanced, therefore more productive (Time Magazine 18th of March 2013)[68].

Globalization allows almost everybody to work around the clock. I run my websites and work with people in different time zones. I could work 15 hours a day every single day without any difficulty, being on my own, and changing hats according to needs. Doing so makes no sense to me, however, because I have a life outside my job; I have a family. In addition, my job is about boosting long-term relationships. If I don't walk the road I preach, there is a problem, don't you think? Does not working all hours affect my business negatively? It is hard to tell. But to be honest, it does not really matter to me. I strongly believe that I work enough to make it a success if it is meant to be. I know deep inside that I can't force people to take care of their relationships if they are not ready to do so. I don't work with assumptions in mind; I work with integrity and the deep belief that what I do has some value. I don't want my business to run me.

---

68 http://www.ezcouple.com/beincharge

Many people who work so-called high profile jobs are totally infatuated with their own importance. When I was working as an intern at a high-end law firm in Paris, I would arrive at 7:45AM ready to work but most partners and associates would come at 9AM, and start with a coffee. I would take 30 minutes for lunch but they would take a good hour and sometimes more. Their working energy would only really kick in at 3:30PM or 4PM, with the peak at 6PM and the workday day ending at 10:30PM, sometimes later. Many of these lawyers were divorced; their life was their work. Did they use their time efficiently? I don't believe so. Long hours often result in inefficiency at some point: people worked absurd hours because everyone else did, they all thought they were expected to.

Women are deeply aware of efficiency issues, yet they comply with workplace norms or expectations. I guess that when you are not lucky enough to work for someone like Hillary Clinton in Washington DC, you have little choice but to comply. Read former Under Secretary of State and business leader Charlotte Beers's book, I'd Rather Be In Charge[69] to find out if you ladies in the work place stay true to yourself and fully express your potential. Charlotte Beers' book offers a self-assessment that will teach you a lot about yourself at work and beyond. Women's insecurity is a plague that hinders life at all levels. I also believe that this insecurity is the basis of many relationship problems. A sense of inferiority can trigger scorekeeping over who does what, as if this game truly valued what women do on a daily basis.

It is important to become aware of the amazing skills particular to the female mind that could benefit the world. Men would be better off adding these skills to their own arsenal. Let's explore what is so special about women. Often women are declared "complex." Why is that? The best way to understand this complexity is to analyze two

<hr>

69 http://www.ezcouple.com/beincharge

physical characteristics unique to any woman's body: the bundle of fluctuating hormones meant to prepare a body for pregnancy every month, and the body itself with one additional opening, in the groin area, barely protected. It is essential to realize that a woman's mind is closely influenced by these two factors. Fluctuating hormones cause all sorts of mood swings totally out of her control or will power. And these barely protected openings in the body affect a woman's sense of safety and cleanliness at a deep level.

To start with, let's talk about **hormones**. If men had the slightest idea what it is to go through a cycle of hormones the way we do every month, there would definitely be less potential for gender conflict during that time each month. What makes monthly periods unwelcome is that our male-dominated world has flattened everything according to a male perspective. So characteristics that are unfamiliar to men are not welcome. This is especially true when these characteristics affect the rhythm, the pace of life. Of course, men's hormones are not totally stable either; in fact they are highly sensitive to stress. But the cycle men go through does not follow an obvious monthly rhythm so it can simply be overlooked. It is therefore difficult for them to understand what the women's experience of monthly cycles is like. For the past 50 years, women have infiltrated the male-dominated business world by masking and overlooking the characteristics of the female cycle. Women have felt the need to act like men in order to be respected in the work place. The problem is that neither is sustainable in the long run. A conventional perspective blames men because some of them still refuse to respect women who would be too "girly." I believe the responsibility should be shared. Only women can identify their disconnection from themselves, and no one knows better than they what is needed to restore that connection. Every woman's energy level is subject to a sinusoidal cycle of hormones. The bottom of the sinusoid is the menstruation: energy is dedicated to this cleansing process, and it is normal to feel less energetic during the process. As the workplace has become more demanding for everybody, women are often in the position of not being able to feel and respect this cycle, and they cope by engaging their adrenal system instead, therefore raising their stress level. Over time, mind and body start aching as a result of this disrespect, and soon aches and pains plague the body, and depression and hysteria plague the mind. This is particularly true when a woman has gone through pregnancy and delivery of a baby. It takes nine months for the body to conceive and have a baby ready to be born, and yet nobody finds it strange that a woman is expected to be back to her original state in less than three months. Nature's laws are consistent. Common sense would recommend that if something takes nine months to be created, the "undoing" should not take less time. A revolution has occurred inside the body to accept and nourish a foreign body for nine months. Learn about the difficulties encountered during and after organ transplants in order to understand the scope of this perfectly natural miracle. A similar revolution to pregnancy, in reverse, starts right after delivery and lasts several months, if all goes well. Considering how closely the female mind is linked to a woman's hormonal system, respecting and understanding the instability following delivery makes a difference in a woman's well-being. In ignoring this, we make here the same mistake we make with so many medical treatments: we take action on the symptoms when they start bothering us, ignoring the fact that symptoms are the tip of an iceberg that has been building over a long period of time. Relieving only the symptoms not only gives us a false sense of health, but it may hinder our access to true health because it disconnects us from the warnings the body gives when it's in distress. If your foot hurts, you will spontaneously stand and walk less to decrease the pain. When you take medication to deaden the pain and carry on your usual activity forgetting your foot, and its call for rest, the inflammation gets worse. Your body compensates by requiring additional work from your other foot, and your knees and hips, and you end up with pain on both sides, requiring more medication. The vicious cycle has started. I am not saying that pain medication should be avoided at all costs, as I well know that it is sometimes necessary to keep us sane. I just think it should not be a reflex, like fever medication given for the slightest fever. Fever, coughing, and pain are signals that something is wrong. It is better to take care of what is wrong before suppressing the symptoms. In any case, symptoms will cease by themselves once the root cause is addressed. What happens with women is no different. Although birth control is still a major step in liberating women, birth control pills, in particular, have disconnected women from their true selves, artificially creating cycles that depend on artificial chemicals. For those of you who take the Pill for medical reasons other than birth control, please know that there are other options worth for you to investigate. The side effects of these pills go far beyond breast tenderness, cysts, or other nodules. They wreak havoc on our fragile, super-sensitive hormonal system, affecting our mood as well. The relationship between mood and hormone imbalance is similar to that between the chicken and the egg: which came first, therefore causing the other to exist? Here again a vicious cycle is initiated. Do you know how sensitive and intuitive the hormonal system of a woman is? If you don't already know this, you may be surprised to see that it is true: if several women live under the same roof, if they are free of any type of medication regulating their hormonal system, within a few months their menstruation will come at the same time of the month. Martha McClintock[70], the first person to document that scientifically, wrote the

---

70 http://www.ezcouple.com/mmclintock

first article about it in Nature in 1971, "Menstrual Synchronicity and Suppression." Later, she and others established that this synchronicity was caused by pheromones. What is interesting to understand here is that women are connected to one another to an extent we might not expect. In addition, it means that the usual need to withdraw we all have during our period should not be understood as a need for isolation. We are just meant to be with other women with whom our energy level will resonate during that time. Physically we are also meant to keep any male at a distance at that time, so whether we like it or not, it is not going to be a time we can be nice and understanding with our male partner. The fact that a majority of women use birth control pills, though, changes that dynamic because the cycle is then artificial. The Pill masks sensitivity to body signals.

Women connect with everything through their body. Their bodily sensitivity is the antenna that places them in tune with the universe, with the unseen. The extraordinary ability all women have to perceive the unseen, and sense the danger way before it happens should not be ignored the way it has been so far. The subtlety of this sense has to be valued in order to be useful. Its reliability depends on the stillness of the mind and the ability to call upon it on a regular basis. Stress shuts down our subtle perceptions. These perceptions are receptors for a wisdom that goes beyond all human beings. They are this connection between the past and the future. Women should be listened to, even though they know things without knowing how they know them. It is hard for us to trust intuition when it has been ridiculed, ignored, and despised for a long time. But it only takes us deciding to listen to, and trust what we hear and feel; and with practice it will be spontaneous. What men do not realize is that with you, ladies, they have a super-sensitive scanner, antenna, or radar at their disposal. Women perfectly complement men, being able to put things in perspective for them in a way men don't have access to.

Another characteristic that has significant consequences is that women have more unprotected **openings in their body**, than men do. The female body has three openings in the groin area that need to be particularly clean therefore we need to pay more attention to them than other body parts. We all attend to these parts so unconsciously that we forget how unique and important they are in our day. First, let's be honest, we need to urinate more. Unlike men, we have nothing that stops the law of gravity to apply when our smaller bladder is full. Hence we go to the bathroom more often…and we stay longer. Yes, gentlemen, we have nothing to shake, and here we go! Necessarily, ladies take more time to go to the bathroom, and the bathroom's cleanliness is more important to them. We need to be cleaner because bacteria and other viruses could easily enter our body through these openings. This is one of the reasons why women are more prone to urinary tract infections than men. By extension, a woman's house is treated just like her body. Keeping it clean and tidy is critical. So the next time she fusses about tidiness and cleanliness, be nice, gentlemen: she needs that cleanliness to feel comfortable. So do it for her. Nowadays, with the pace of life, these needs are stressful! Which may provide some clues as to why women are more prone to depression. Many of them cope with their lives by taking anti-depressants. In the twenty years since 1988, the use of antidepressants across all ages in America has increased nearly 400 percent, according to the Centers for Disease Control and Prevention website[71]. Women are two and a half time more likely to take antidepressant than men. Whether anti-depressants are rightly prescribed or not, the need for anti-depressants is worrisome. This is a sign that something is deeply wrong with the way we live, don't you think? What if, instead,

71 http://www.ezcouple.com/cdc3

women reconnected with their body, enjoying massages on a regular basis, connecting with girlfriends regularly, and taking time off? That sounds like a delusional paradise in today's life, I know. But it may not seem so unrealistic if we take some common sense steps that all religions have taken into account for a long time. Religious communities all have one day a week dedicated to rest and prayer. This is a true day off for everyone. Do we all have to turn to religion to have one day of a week respected and not challenged? How long will it take before we understand that the alternating night and day is here for a reason? In this world of one-size-fits-all, dominated by our children's desire for immediate gratification, and by multitasking beyond human processing capabilities, it is time to get back to some kind of rhythm, starting with our schedule. It wouldn't reduce women's efficiency at work: if they feel they make a difference, they will never abuse the flexibility that allows them to respect their rhythm. If you look closely, most women are astonishingly efficient and proactive. That will not change.

The question is then how to balance our hormones so we stay tuned into our wisdom and don't feel like a yo-yo all the time, one day in tears and the next euphoric. Men may complain that they don't see much of the euphoria; very often, an excited form of hysteria has replaced euphoria.

The answer to this is necessarily convoluted. I believe the best first step is to have our hormones regularly checked while keeping our stress level under control. Both men and women need to check that their hormones are in order if they want to have any sex life at all. Testosterone, or the lack of it for women should I say, plays a major role in women's interest in sex, and for men its influence goes way beyond the sex drive. Stress and food also have an impact on men's hormones as well but overall their hormones are fairly stable.

Women's hormones, however, are disrupted very easily. It is frequent that women after pregnancy have trouble getting back to a normal hormonal cycle. Just a quick thought on pregnancy: this specific time in a woman's life is a major disrupter totally overlooked by the medical staff after delivery. According to them, as long as the new mom is able to have sex without pain within six weeks of delivery, she is good to go. No woman feels "normal" after six weeks, and yet they are told that they are fine. And we wonder why so many mothers experience post-partum depression!

The next step would be to look at what you eat, and make sure you are well informed on the estrogen hidden in your food (in soy, milk, and meat for instance). Girls start puberty younger and younger now, causing all sorts of psychological problems, and yet we hardly hear about the connection of that to our food. The milk that most kids are fed from a young age, in particular, is stuffed with hormones. Hormones in food send messages to the endocrine system of the body that disrupt the production and release of hormones. The internet is filled with documentation on the toxicity of certain foods for the hormonal system: you can check the <u>Agency for Toxic Substances & Disease Registry's website</u>[72] to find official data on the matter.

Another step is to make sure fluids keep moving within your body. Hydration is, of course, a key factor in increasing blood volume, hydrating the very demanding brain, and keeping constipation at bay. Massages have been used for centuries across all cultures as a healing tool: they stimulate the body's elimination of toxins by helping blood circulation. They also relax the mind enabling the lymphatic system to work properly. Gentle, superficial strokes performed in a certain way will activate the precious lymphatic system, the primary barrier in our immune system. In Orange County, California <u>Marilyn Mercado</u>[73]

72 http://www.ezcouple.com/atsdr
73 http://www.ezcouple.com/lymph

provides state of the art lymphatic drainages: you can check her site for more information.

Last but not least, we must work on our mood. The more we do the things we love, the more we read inspiring books, novels, or listen to music, the less likely we will perpetuate a vicious cycle in which our mood perpetuates a chemical imbalance.

We should never forget that our body is the precious home for the soul. We must nurture it, take care of it, and respect it if we want it to serve us well.

Part 3: A Working Woman Is A Better Deal For Everyone

Thanks to the "Adam and Eve" story, women having power just like men is unconsciously, or consciously, seen as dangerous. However, it is the road back to balance that may save us all from the unpleasant consequences of irresponsible economic growth. The ordeal of former stay-at-home mothers who must look for a job has to stop. Stay-at-home mothers develop amazing skills that should certainly be valued when they look for a job. It is so irritating for me to see that the only way for a woman who has put her career on hold to raise her children to get a decent job is to be self- employed. There are exceptions of course, but the rule in the western world is that to be employed in leading jobs, you need to be "plug and play." This expression is commonly used in the business world to define a recruitment profile for a specific job: a person is said to be "plug and play" when she has done the exact same job in a different firm. By definition, a mother who has been home to raise her family is never "plug and play." Her ability to learn and perform in the work place is often underestimated. A woman who has been able to safely raise one or several human beings from infancy through adulthood has MANY skills. Children are the best trainers ever! They challenge you every single day when you least expect to be challenged. Let me list skills a stay-at-home mom necessarily develops; they should certainly be appealing to any employer:

Leadership: Do you know what it takes nowadays to convince children, a husband, contractors, or employees to do something? Without a minimum of leadership, a stay-at-home mom would never get anything done.

Flexibility: As long as you have to deal with several people all day long, especially immature ones, you develop an amazing ability to adjust to different approaches. In addition, a mother is constantly interrupted by the urgent needs of her children, and very often she has to delay or postpone what she initially planned to do.

Great communication skills: Throughout the day, a stay-at-home mom speaks at least four languages: the husband's language, contractors' languages, women's language, and children's language (knowing that each age has its own dialect!)

Outstanding multi-tasking: Pay a visit to any household with children between 6:30pm and 8:30pm and you will see an amazing multi-tasker in action: the mom! She baths the kids, prepares dinner, helps with homework, tidies up behind them, and fights against her children's reluctance to start their bedtime routine, all at the same time.

Thoroughness: Of course all mothers choose their battles to keep their sanity, but there is always at least one thing they are very thorough about.

Ability to negotiate and compromise: Feeding a child with something healthful from the age he is able to complain about it and resist is an efficient way to develop your negotiating skills. Although the "best" parenting techniques tell you that it is wrong to do so, I do not know one parent who does not make deals with their children: "If you eat this, you will get that very appealing thing…" Nowadays parents negotiate everything with their kids…or I should say: children negotiate everything with their parents.

Dedication and Hard work: Everybody knows that a stay-at-home mom's day starts when she wakes up and finishes when she goes to bed. Do you need more?

Creativity: Children these days get bored three seconds after being left with an unguided activity other than screen time. To find the next thing to do, who do they go to? Mom. She needs to be resourceful to meet that challenge every day.

Ability to handle emergencies effectively: Once again, check how efficient and responsive mothers are in dealing with accidents that end up in emergency rooms to find out how well mothers, even super-stressed, deal with any kind of emergencies.

The only business sense a mom does not have is a good sense of her own value in the business world. A former stay-at-home mom looking for a job should be viewed as a great asset for any employer.

Many people believe that working women are a symptom of economic and political crisis. They should therefore be viewed as an abnormality: the norm being for women to be confined to domestic roles. It is true that women started to climb the business ladder during war times when there were no men to provide, and women had to jump into the workforce to fill the gaps. In fact many women work today because one salary is not enough to provide for the family. Crises always bring changes, and very often these changes are for the better. The so-called norm well served a society based on males in absolute power; it does not serve a society based on mutual respect and love. I will opt for the feminist view here; these crises gave women the opportunity to finally understand that they can make decisions for themselves outside the household. If, at first sight, the professional woman seems like a major challenge for any relationship, it is in fact the opportunity to build the foundations of a healthy, balanced relationship.

Many people find working women to be the root cause of the relationship crisis. If we want our daughters to start a family in the future we had better break this belief. Many people think that a stay-at-mom relieves tensions in a marriage. A woman who is totally – and only – dedicated to their family, is an obsolete concept. And I truly believe this is for the best. Why is it obsolete? First, financially, very few families can afford to have a stay-at-home mom. Expenses don't stop rising when incomes are, at best, staying level. Without doing anything fancy, most couples need two salaries to cope with their expenses. Second, you can't expect a highly educated woman to enjoy ignoring the education that she gained all day long. Sooner or later, she will feel that she has sacrificed her career, and her life, for the sake of her husband and kids. And when she finally has the time to consider a career after 10 or 15 years of being a stay-at-home mom, her degrees have almost no value. She is then stuck with a market value that is close to zero, and that is legitimately unacceptable. These women's difficulties will then also become their husband's at a time when he is not in the best position either, unless he is a successful business owner. Besides, it is extremely frustrating for a woman to be dependent on a man at a time when job stability is close to none.

Last and most important, we need women in the work environment, in politics, and anywhere else major decisions are made. Men and women are different and complementary; the more they will work together the better for all. In developed civilizations women have gained an expanded view of the world, and they have the opportunity to express their unique skills throughout it. This is a wonderful thing. A woman who works is under a lot of pressure, and has less time; that is for sure! And she very often deals with two days instead of one, one at work and one at home. So, is she stressed? Yes, indeed. Is the solution to bring her back home? Certainly not.

Let me explain. Her work is a critical part of her balance. Her job makes her feel alive and self-reliant. In this world where community and family have been reduced to their nucleus, for woman, working is a way to be part of that world. It is a way to count and make things move. I believe that working women have better self-esteem than women who don't because they have a social role to play that is recognized. Does that mean that stay-at-home moms are socially useless? Definitely not! In fact, they have the most difficult job: their day never ends, they work non-stop from morning to night. They don't get any salary for that either, so they rely on their partner financially. They are responsible for their children full time. And if you have children, you know how difficult it is to raise children these days. In addition, most stay-at-home moms do charity work at their children's school or elsewhere.

From the perspective of a partner though, it is not a good deal to have a stay-at-home mom as a partner: She will expect, only from him, recognition and acknowledgement, and more or less acknowledgement depending on her self-esteem. And guess what? After a day at work, the last thing that comes to a man's mind is to praise his wife because their home is tidy and clean, because a meal is ready for him, because his shirts are all back from the dry cleaner ...and so on. First, he is tired and all he wants is to be able to relax in front of TV. The only thing that could motivate him at that time is sex. Well, sex is probably the last thing on her mind after fixing dinner, getting the kids showered, cleaning up after them, and preparing school lunches for the next day. (I always wonder where guys got the idea that domestic duties could ever possibly turn any woman on!)

Does he get any praise from earning money that sustains the family life style every day? No. He does his job. So does she! The only difference is that he can be praised at work through a promotion or salary increase, or even a simple compliment from his boss or a client. She rarely gets any praise ever. Children nowadays, more so than ever, consider that whatever she does is totally normal, expected and due. And considering how hard he works, the husband is not far from agreeing with the children. As unselfish and dedicated as women can be, this arrangement does not work. Or if it works, soon it won't. At some point, she will be sick and tired of being the dependent one, the one her own children will look down on when they are aiming for those great careers that mom can't possibly have any clue about! Or so they believe!

In our culture, independence is financial independence before anything else. Depending on somebody is fine, but it does not suggest a fully mature person. Even if you have the most delightful, understanding, and generous husband, if he is the breadwinner, his spending choices will prevail over yours. In times of recession, this is even more true because ultimately he is the one who decides, being the one who makes the money. Interestingly, when I was in Singapore, I saw the opposite situation where a wife was working full-time while the husband was at home taking care of the family. This couple seemed to be working well. He was an exceptional man with little ego and solid self-esteem. And she seemed quite exceptional, too, praising his skills in taking care of the house and the children.

In America, according to the latest census, it is a rising trend for men to stay home while the wife works. There were an estimated 176,000 stay-at-home dads in 2011. How that is going to evolve, I am not sure. The few men I know in this situation are not there by choice. And they would much rather have a "proper" job. <u>The New-York Times</u>[74] presents a different perspective in this article, with dads perfectly happy being home, and considering themselves the new norm. It is a good opportunity for men to picture exactly what is asked of their wives under similar circumstances… Yet, I would not consider stay-at-home dads the new norm because it looks to me like another extreme. Men can be excellent fathers while also working outside the home. Whether a man or a woman, a good parent does not have to be dedicated 24/7 to their child: in my experience, the more adults that a child sees the better.

While it is true to say that a woman who has a job has more external pressure than the one who does not, there are many benefits to the fact that she works besides those stated above. For the husband in particular, one benefit is that the wife has a better understanding of what his life is like, and more importantly, how stressed he can be. Therefore, she necessarily "nags" less. Nagging is one of the primary complaints men in a long-term relationship have. To a woman, nagging is nothing more than repeating herself. A woman who works will use at home more of the type of communication she would use at work. Communication in the work environment is very often male: that means that messages are straightforward, using no circumlocution. Communication is very direct.

Another benefit is that she feels entitled to do more; she is more self-reliant. In addition, the couple enjoys more financial freedom, which gives them the opportunity "to throw money" at domestic issues to sort them out. This is a big stress reliever! Last but not least, what a great example she gives to her kids! Gentlemen, for those of you who are working your head off to save for your daughter's college, don't

---

74 http://www.ezcouple.com/nyt0812

you see how contradictory it can be to push your child to study well to get admitted to a top college when you are perfectly happy with her mom staying at home and serving you? Let me throw in an anecdote that happened many years ago in Singapore when my eldest child was in kindergarten. It was at the end of a school day; several of us mothers were waiting for our respective child. When the kids joined us we were discussing jobs/careers; naturally one of the moms asked the kids what they would want to be in the future. To this day I think we all remember the answer of this little girl, my son's age: "I want to be a nothing like my mom." The mother, who had to give up a job in California to follow her husband to Singapore, felt outraged and hurt. How could a six-year-old consider a stay-at home mom a nothing? I still wonder.

For the moment it is true that for most women working means struggling to combine their career and their personal life, but it would be manageable and fulfilling if the stress was under control. And when the stress is under control, these women will not only be a great role model for their daughters, they will also be fun partners, both emotionally and physically.

Part 4: Women Must Go Beyond Their Fears

It is about time we think harder to make sure our daughters have a better life than we do.

In the western world, women's situation has never been better. We can vote. We can study, work, and aim for the top positions politically and in business organizations. The reality, though, is in the numbers.

Sheryl Sandberg, COO of Facebook, talks much better than I about these numbers, and I really encourage you to view her Ted Talk video[75], which you can watch on my blog. I am glad she wrote "Lean In: Women, Work, and the Will to Lead"[76] and started an association to nurture women's leadership. I wish, though, she was clear about what it takes on a personal level: it takes childcare and domestic help. No woman with children takes a high profile position in the work place without that. Superwoman does not exist. What is interesting in Anne-Marie Slaughter's criticism of Sheryl Sandberg's theory is that she repeats that it is delusional for highly-educated women aiming for top positions to believe they can have it all. It really depends on what we consider having it all. If having it all is to be a high achiever at work, super mom, and super wife, then, no, it is not possible.

The thing is that everything is flawed in the previous sentence: high achiever is a concept from the nineties that places jobs on a corporate ladder that is currently being drastically revolutionized by both technology and globalization. Listen to Seth Godin[77] interviewed by Krista Tippett on her radio show "On Being" to understand his realistic view of the marketplace right now. Super mothers are suffocating, and, as a result of being the decision maker at all times for their kids, when their children get to college they are unable to decide for themselves. I was told of one young man in his first college year who had to call his mother to decide whether he should eat this or that. It may sound extreme, and hopefully this is the exception and not the rule. The super wife died in the 70s when women stopped torturing themselves to appear pampered at all times for their man's pleasure.

However, if having it all means being able to have a family while having a career without feeling overstretched, then it is possible, with drastic change in the work place starting from the top. Gradually

75 http://www.ezcouple.com/blogvid1
76 http://www.ezcouple.com/leanin
77 http://www.ezcouple.com/nprob6

women leaders will bring some sanity into the work place that will leave more room for a family. This is precisely what Sheryl Sandberg would like to do. Sandberg leaves Facebook at 5:30pm, and it is not the end of the world. Hillary Clinton started officially to work from 8am to 7pm to make sure her staff had a family life. Mark Zuckerberg even says that he ceased to be hungry most of the day since Sandberg joined Facebook because he does not skip lunch anymore (Time Magazine 18th of March 2013)[78].

What most people don't see in the media excitement around the debate confronting two visions of high-achieving women is that Sheryl Sandberg has two kids and the eldest is 7, while Anne-Marie Slaughter has two teenagers. Teenagers can be far more challenging to our emotional balance, especially when you have a 14-year-old who does not see the fantastic opportunities we work hard to display before him. I totally relate to that, having a 14-year-old son myself who had much rather play League of Legends with his friends than do his homework. It is both frightening and extremely stressful for parents, and it is easy for a mom to feel responsible when she works far from her home. Truth be told, isn't it part of being a teenager to reject conventions and what parents and adults suggest as right? Have we all forgotten? We are so anxious about the fact that Junior might miss his college opportunities because in 9th grade, a student's record starts to matter. We all have the friend whose teenager studies super well with personal ambition as a drive. So anxiety quickly becomes panic because we don't want our child to be left behind. Of course parenting then takes another direction that Sheryl Sandberg might have difficulty grasping at her stage of parenthood. Nevertheless Sheryl Sandberg is still right: we need to have more women in leading positions to change habits in the work place. And I am close to thinking that we

78 http://www.ezcouple.com/time0313

need to relax a bit regarding our teenagers. Easier said than done, I know. More parenting is not necessarily going to solve anything, and a job is what might get you through those years without losing total control of your own sanity. The teenage phase is difficult no matter what, for everybody. As long as communication is still open, the best attitude is probably not the interventionist one. The reality is that working mothers are consumed with guilt that serves no one. The second strongest pressure on all women's shoulders is appearance. It is not so much the fact that women pay attention to themselves that is highlighted here. It is the reason why we do it. Women must seduce and convince, and their appearance is key in the process. It is precisely this reason that places men in a different position far less pressurized when it comes to the way they look. This necessity for women to seduce and convince is such an old pattern that it invariably sticks in our collective belief system. It directly affects the way a woman is perceived and most importantly, how she feels about herself. It is hard to change patterns that have been going on for centuries.

Poor self-confidence in most women is linked to the fact that, for a very long time, women have seen themselves through men's eyes. I was looking at the old TV show "Bewitched" with my daughter the other day. And suddenly, while watching Samantha's submissive attitude towards her husband, I understood why unconsciously I had banned all pink and girly stuff for my daughter, who, as a result, has never played dolls, princess, or anything like that. I guess I had the unconscious conviction that this was a misleading definition of what it means to be a girl. I find it difficult shopping for gifts for girls because I do not want to feed into this debilitating, servile drive to confine women to an obedient domestic role. If we want the male-female interaction to change, it has to start in education. It has to start in our homes. Who would offer a doll or an ironing board to a boy? Who would offer cars, or power symbols to a girl?

My little boy, when he was five, loved to dress up a baby doll neglected by my daughter, but very quickly peer pressure taught him that it was not cool to do so, for a boy: it was a girl thing! How much longer will learning to care for others stay primarily a girl thing? Most of the best teachers my kids have had were male teachers; they were all very diligent about teaching respect between genders, and teaching girls and boys to work together. It is stunning to me to see how it is, here in South California. From a very early age, boys are encouraged to socialize with boys only, and idem for girls. How come we don't see how deeply wrong this is? Women and men are very different, so are boys and girls. This is the reason why we need to put more effort into making sure they acclimate and understand one another in a respectful way. Why not pair a boy and a girl at school for all collective tasks? When boys and girls play separately from kindergarten, how can we expect a deep, natural male-female mutual understanding later on in life?

When I finished the equivalent of fifth grade in France, I changed schools. I was, along with twenty-two other girls, the first generation of female students in a 50-year-old boys' school. To "survive" in that male dominated environment, we, the girls, had to review our behaviors and our way of thinking. Boys were playing games that were new to us. We had to be as good as they were to be included, even if they had been playing these games for a long time and we had just started. Personally, it was not difficult; I loved boys' games. I found them much more fun than anything the girls did. That experience probably shaped me much more than I have ever been aware of. I guess my initial interest in the male's mind took root then.

I believe, today, that we need to create balanced communication between men and women. We also need to restore healthy relationships between women as well, and mutual respect between those who don't work and those who work, between those with leading positions, and the others. The insecurity most women feel hinders their relationship not only with men but also with other women. As a result, women are not helping one another the way they could. At the rate we are going, we might as well be dead and our children too, before male-female equality is the norm at home and at work.

Collective patterns are very hard to change. Before we blame men for not changing fast enough, we should review our own behavior first. We need more and more women in the workforce, especially in leading positions. Personal fulfillment that does not necessarily involve motherhood is critical for most women, and this is healthy. It is healthy for them, and for the world, because it fosters ethics and values in the business world. A woman who has children will be less likely to make decisions that could potentially harm her children in the long run. Most men compartmentalize their lives so well that in the workplace they totally forget that they are fathers. The world needs more women in power. Relationships need the commitment of self-reliant women who want to make it work, so relationships can last in the 21st century and beyond.

Imagine how the workplace would look if women in leading positions had a fulfilling personal life as well. Respect would be a core value. For this goal, we must support one another. We should not feel threatened by the appearance or the success of another woman. We are no longer in competition to get the full attention of a male for our future survival. Our daughters will seize the opportunity that was offered to us, to be fully financially independent from the start: they will choose their male partner because they want a fulfilling personal life, not because they have to have a male partner. Raising children should be a manageable part of a fulfilling life. I keep repeating that a day is 24 hours long no matter what. It is unsustainable to ask a woman to have two, sometimes three jobs a day. You know that I am adamant about domestic help, believing it is a necessity to keep all sanity.

I also think that more interactions with other women would lower the stress level of many women. Women benefit from talking to one another. Even John Gray in his most recent book, <u>Venus on Fire Mars on Ice</u>[79], says so. Never in human history has raising a child fallen on the shoulders of one person only. If you take a look at traditional communities, as soon as the children are weaned, the entire community raises the children. So why are we waiting to increase the mutual help we can offer each other? Take carpools as a practical example, so often neglected. Why are there so few carpools? Here is my explanation: Women, after freeing themselves more or less successfully from a male tutorial system, have submitted to the dictatorship of their own children. They let those they should guide be the guide. They follow their kids' agenda relentlessly. I am close to believing that there is a conspiracy to make sure that women never reach their full potential.

Once you have a child these days, know that crystal is easier to take care of. The mother is held responsible for the child's physical health, his mental health, his development, his growth, and his attitude. Children are treated like mini adults with full rights. In fact the child has more rights than the mother has. He can traumatize her by driving her insane, but she can't take any measures to protect herself because this is bad parenting. This child needs to express himself, he needs to be heard, he needs to be acknowledged every minute, even if the child has no sense of boundaries, and tramples other people's personal space repeatedly. A child is self-centered, which is part of being a child. As a result he is completely selfish, and

79 http://www.ezcouple.com/Gray

that selfishness should be gradually weeded out if we eventually want to make a responsible and caring adult out of that child. Children are not the fragile creatures, easily traumatized, that most parenting lecturers will claim they are. If that were the case, we would not exist. How could our great grandparents, grandparents, or even our parents have coped with the dreadful childhood they had when they were neither seen nor heard? Children are growing beings; they need love and assistance until their brain is fully developed. So, can we stop pretending that these little beings have the ability to decide for themselves?

The worst stage is teenage years. It seems that the more research being done on these transitional years, the less common sense we use in dealing with them. Teenagers are deceptive because they very quickly look like grown-ups even if their brain is still a child's brain. How can we expect a teenager to make the right decision for his own sake when he does not have the brain to do so? To be precise I should say the frontal lobe of a teenager's brain, the Jiminy Cricket of the brain, is (only) partially connected, making that teenager unable to make sound decisions for himself. Read the interesting story of neuroscientist Frances Jensen, confronted by the dilemma parents face with a teenager. Richard Knox, who tells the story on npr.org[80], describes really well this helplessness and hopelessness parents feel with their teenage children while detailing the scientific explanations for those interactions. Let's get back to those years when our child is not yet a complete alien. Respecting to the letter what our child says and supposedly feels, we won't carpool if the child does not want to. It does not matter that it saves you precious time to carpool; it does not matter if it is a critical help in another parent's life. We won't put up a fight, one more, for carpooling.

---

80 http://www.ezcouple.com/npr

Are we all mad???

We should not let the children rule our lives. It is detrimental to us and to them. Ladies, friends, the alternative is this: either we find a way to bring back balance into our lives or we stop having children altogether. For those of us who already have children, there is no alternative: we must find a way! Ladies, we should get together; we should be kind to one another; we should try to make our lives easier, and we should help one another, so we can all express our potential. The time is right: many women and men will welcome us on this path.

7

THE WAY TO GO FOR A HEALTHY RELATIONSHIP

A healthy relationship is one in which both partners find fulfillment. It does not mean that the road is always smooth, but overall both are willing to stay. Respect is its core value: there is no such thing as love without respect. And it all starts with self-respect. Kindness, understanding, generosity, the ability to help, and compassion are not sustainable in the long run without self-respect. Always start with yourself before attending to others: neglecting yourself serves no one.

Part 1: Respect And Embrace Your Calling!

Too often, people dismiss their callings just because they are not in line with other people's expectations. Callings can't be in line with anyone else's expectations for one good reason: they have a purpose in the future. So most callings will not find much support and very often others will be hostile to them. Take J.K. Rowling, who had to send her manuscript to many editors before one would consider publishing Harry Potter, or Henry Ford, with his V8 engine, who was perceived as a joke until he built that engine. More recently, Steve Jobs is another striking example. Callings are not the latest fad that will dissipate over time. They are more like percolating, recurrent thoughts. You don't even know where your calling will lead you, but you keep moving towards it because it feels right. Men have always been encouraged to be adventurous and try things out, while women were bred to be docile and conventional. Inevitably, women are less likely to follow their calling than men because tons of reasons come their way to stop them. So, ladies, you must follow your calling, and put your fear of failure aside. Failure is part of the process. Let's pause one moment and consider fear of failure, a fear that is usually linked to fear of rejection. These fears can literally paralyze anybody. And yet, failure is the most efficient learning process available to human kind. There is plenty to learn from a failure. And if you manage to successfully quiet your panicking little ego, you will grow from that experience. After a failure, the question is always should I quit or not? First, no project is brought to life without bumps and holes where it looks like the project might be just dead. Perseverance, motivated by enormous drive, is usually what successfully brings the project to life. That does not necessarily mean that quitting is a coward move. All projects big or small require a lot of energy day after day. Your project has to resonate with you; if it does not, then it is better to quit. Whatever you did fuels a thinking process and a set of emotional tools that will prove useful in the future when you least expect it. There is no such thing as wasting time, because a calling always comes at the right time in your life. On the other hand, if you still find inside you something that pushes you to stay and fight, by all means, follow that voice. Even if it does not make sense to others, even if it does not really make sense to you, stay with your project. It will eventually make sense. The media overwhelm us with success stories without sharing the path that has led to success. That path is never a smooth ride: risks are taken, doubts are lingering, blockages have to be overcome, and decisions have to be made with limited awareness of the consequences. Of course, all these bumps and blocks are glamorous and romantic once success is there. But until then …it is not an easy road. And you will find well-intentioned people who will warn you by pointing out the millions of reasons your project will never meet with success, to spare you from the adverse effects of failure. As I am still in the startup phase of EZcouple, without any guarantee that it will be a success, I can tell you that I know what perseverance means, and what it is to have this little voice inside that keeps you going, and this other voice that tells you to be careful. Always trust yourself, and see what happens. All projects big or small have the value you give to them. Of course, anybody would much rather have a project worth millions, but ultimately what counts is the psychological fulfillment one gets from it. Often, although the partner's support is badly needed, it's lacking. Fear is at the root of the problem, with fear of rejection a primary one. What will people think? This is the characteristic question linked to the fear of rejection. Many callings require life adjustments that change our routine while also shaking our belief system. Certainty is foreign in the process of finding and following a calling. The opposite is in fact the norm: it takes a huge amount of will power and determination that is sustainable only if there is someone next to you to support you when doubts arise. Doubts always come at one point or the other, especially when you face a form of rejection. Novelty is always fought against initially because it disturbs the skeptics; all callings are bound to face rejection at some point. Most people only approve projects after they receive confirmation from a majority. Until then, we are on our own, facing indifference or worse, open rejection. Although we might be aware of it, it is never pleasant. In truth it might be really painful. If we don't want the pain to distract us from our goal, we need an external help that will put things in perspective for us, and remind us how loved, and therefore loveable, we are. If our partner has a calling, we must rely on the trust and love we have for him or her to help when it is needed. We are the only one who is able to provide ongoing support. Remember how many exemplary men in the past have admitted their wife was critical in their success. We must support our partner in his or her pursuit, either to find the calling or to follow it. Callings do not happen overnight. They take time and reflection to reach our awareness.

There are many advantages in being with someone who has found his or her calling. The passion of living something meaningful will nurture the love that your understanding and support foster. In addition, our partner can be an essential catalyst when he or she offers praise and encouragement. Along the way, he or she is the precious confidante who can lovingly put us back on the right track whenever we get dragged in the wrong direction. I can't tell you how valuable my husband's feedback is to my own experience. I trust him so much that his honest opinion always makes a difference. When you think about it, how many people can you really trust to give you honest feedback on what you do? How many people would dare tell you what they don't like in a loving way? How many could be constructive without any agenda? Whatever we do, it is much easier to have someone on our side who loves us to support us. Gratitude, along with respect, makes the magical recipe for long lasting love.

Part 2: Respect Both Genders' Needs When It Comes To Stress

∽

Men and women handle stress differently, and they rarely stress about the same things. If we understand the dynamic of stress release for men and for women, we are less likely to burden our partner by imposing our own strategy for relief. While women can gain a lot by connecting with other women, men facing stressful situations need to be given a break from any conversation. Encouraging the other to do what provides relief is the best way to keep peace in the family during stressful times.

Let's take a closer look at the dynamic at play when stress is significant. A man feeling stressed will, at the first opportunity, automatically look for what can relieve his tension. My understanding is that two things truly relax men:

• Lying down like a couch potato in front of the TV or the computer with no one to talk to.

• Having sex or exercising.

Usually the woman, the man's partner, immediately perceives his stress, and that triggers her own anxiety. Anxiety in women has two consequences:

• They want to talk about what is wrong.

• Sex is the last thing they want.

As a result, women will either bug their partner to talk about what is bothering them, which is the last thing their partner wants to do, or they will let them be a couch potato until frustration and rebellion kick in later in the evening. Arguments inevitably ensue. Most women would feel deeply offended if their partner came to them with the idea of having sex after he had been a couch potato for hours. This could quickly become a dead-end road for the couple. A long-term relationship is the basis for love and mutual help as long as we respect each partner's individuality.

Whenever the man in the relationship is really stressed, the female partner can use some strategies that will help release his stress.

You, as a woman, have the ability to perceive his anxiety even before he is aware of it. You, therefore, have the ability to lower his stress level before it rises too high. It will be much easier than waiting until he is at his wits' end.

When his stress level is high, you should ask him as little as possible in the evening. He needs that time off to restore his balance. You should get some help with domestic tasks so you don't burn out quickly either. Help can include carpooling, having someone fix dinner, or investing in a <u>Roomba</u>[81], the little round vacuum cleaner that is hypnotic to watch. Use your creativity to find what you need most. Ask your friends, or family to help you out so that it is manageable for you.

At that point your male partner is not the best person to turn to. You won't relieve your own anxiety if you try to talk to him to solve your concerns. If you introduce too many conversations when his stress level is high, you will simply increase his stress level. Not only will your relationship gradually deteriorate, you might also soon have a man with aches and pains. And this is the last straw for your relationship!

---

81 http://www.ezcouple.com/roomba

Women's own strategy for stress management is to talk about their problems, and while doing so a solution sprouts in their mind. They should therefore increase the number of opportunities to talk with their girlfriends. If, on a daily basis, a woman gets enough time to chitchat about her worries with a friend, in stressful times she will not need to have that type of conservation with her male partner in the evening. This is particularly important if a woman wants to be able to provide valuable help to a man who is in a stressful situation. At that point, men are unlikely to be able to provide any help until they restore themselves to an acceptable state of mind.

The priority for the couple is then to understand that the woman is the one who can improve the overall situation for the ultimate benefit of everyone involved. It may seem unfair that the woman has to make the first move and lead the path to recovery, when she is not particularly at ease herself. Yet it is rewarding in the long run because the male partner who has been helped the right way will go the extra mile later on to make his wife happy.

Here is what I think a woman should do in order to help her male partner when he is highly stressed:

Be proactive in taking some time out with him even if you feel he is being unpleasant or boring. Most men when they are highly stressed are self-centered and not particularly attractive. This is the time for true love to come into the picture. You know he is not his usual self; you know he is going through a very difficult time. Put aside the fact that he makes your life dreadful, if that is the case; complain to your mom, your sister, or your best friend if need be, but put it aside when you're together. Perform the ultimate act of love by treating him with care and respect during private time together. As he relaxes, be as loving as you can be; he will open up to you, and you will both feel closer to each other.

Don't try to help him. He already feels terribly guilty for dragging you into his difficulties. The more you show your concern, the worse it will get. So, if you are stressed about money and don't yet work, get a job and find an income. Psychologically you will feel more empowered. Between your job and your home duties, you will have less time to focus on him. Be aware that your focus is perceived as pressure. So less focus on him is less pressure.

Encourage him in what you know are his best assets. Repeat as often as possible how you trust he will do well no matter what he does… even if, at that moment, you don't! Remind him that you love him for who he is, not for his position.

Trust your intuition as to what you feel would be the right move for him, but never choose a time when he feels low to disclose it to him. Try to bring up the subject in the most respectful manner: then he will listen to you, and when he is ready, he will most likely follow your advice.

Lowering your own stress level must be your top priority. Eat well and healthfully, sleep more, exercise, and schedule lunch with friends. Find a spa to go to with a friend to relax fully, and make it a monthly habit or more often if you can.

Last but not least, **stay positive**. With the law of attraction in action, your overall situation should improve, and he will be less likely to be negative. Always remember that life is nothing but cycles. Difficult periods never last forever. Women must proactively take care of their own stress; this is the best way to take good care of others. Often, alas, women are oblivious to their own needs, delaying the right action to an ideal time that never arrives. Men, on the other hand, know quite well how to take care of themselves. They spontaneously do what will relieve their stress, whatever that is. When that consists of having sex, I invite men to be very cautious; in a balanced, healthy relationship a woman can never be used for anything, including sex. Men should never demand sex. It is disrespectful and degrading for the woman. Only prostitutes have sex on demand, and they make a living from it. So unless she is in the mood, the man is better off exercising until he is relaxed enough to make sure sexual intercourse will be a mutual pleasure. Then, and only then is it stress relieving for both. Sex is not on women's radar when they feel stressed. In fact, the pressure to have sex may increase their stress level.

One of the biggest stress relievers for women is to connect with other women. Women benefit from talking and sharing with other women. It seems that this is also a natural way of solving issues. Unfortunately it does not seem to be a priority in today's life. Ladies, do you remember your 20s, when you giggled with your friends and spent hours together talking? Of course you had other things going on, college, a job, or a boyfriend. But not one day would pass without you sharing with a selected few the events or non-events of that day. Then, it was important. These friendships were a priority, and you were so right to think so. More than men do, women need to get together and share time, and talk. The emancipation of women following male rules has slowly but surely isolated women. An independent woman has had to mimic the behavior of an independent man, losing her female connections in the process. It is striking to me to see how difficult it is for women to keep their connections today. Technology provides an amazing tool to ease communication, yet nobody finds the time to make that call, send that email that would nurture friendship. The need to share for women is hormonal: the more women get together and share some time, the lower their stress level is. Therefore, men should encourage that as much as possible.

Why is it so difficult for women to connect with their friends on a regular basis? I see three main reasons for this:

1. Lack of time

2. Difficulty of trust among women

3. General contempt for women's conversations

Increasingly, women's days are filled in such a way that there is no room for anything other than the Have-to's. The Have-to's is my own word describing the "chosen" activities we all have today. We don't really choose the Have-to's; they obey social rules and trends. Women much more than men blindly follow the Have-to's schedule, even if it takes medication for them to cope with their day. Unfortunately, among the Have-to's, there are no girlfriends' gatherings. These are optional, hence rarely in place. And I am not talking about the mom gatherings with several kids around, at which most, if not all conversations revolve around... children and parenting.

We women need two or three good friends with whom we feel comfortable talking freely. The truth is that when you have kids or a job, or both, you already don't have enough time for yourself. So what all or most women who still have a good friend or two do is steal a few minutes over the phone that end up being a good half an hour if not more, in their daily routine. But this way, the phone call leads to guilt if not conflict because it delayed this or that Have-to. I am no exception in this. True time together will never be replaced by a phone call here and there no matter how long it is. In fact for me, it is a problem because most of my friends live very far away. But I make a point of seeing my local friends because I know that it not only nurtures our relationship, but it also lowers my stress level. Even if my schedule is tight like everyone else's, female gatherings are something I do not skip. My priority is always to do everything I can to lower my stress level... without medication!

Besides time constraints, what stops women from getting together on a regular basis is lack of trust. Especially here in America, having a deep, strong relationship with another woman is a challenging task. Fear of judgment and fear of competition are at the root of the unconscious reluctance to share your life with a few other female friends. Once again, this problem comes from adopting a male perspective. When the only way to progress and be acknowledged is to seduce a man who will not only protect you but also give you social status, any other woman is a potential competitor. As a result, anything positive about you, whether it is beauty, intelligence, or kindness, has the seed of feminine rejection within it. Harems fostered this female competition that only benefited the man. Harems have never existed in the western world but male dominance has. And society is still patriarchal today. It would be interesting to see what women's interactions are like in China, where females have been so outnumbered by males since the single-child policy was instituted. Even if China is a strong patriarchal society, the numbers must affect women's confidence in finding the right partner. Choice is on their side.

For centuries, women have had one obsession: securing their future with a suitable marriage. Even worse, until recently, all they could do was seduce the man they wanted, hoping that he would ask her in return to be his wife. You might think that this is really far away from today's reality, but nothing is further from the truth. Psychologically and subconsciously this pattern is still the underlying rule between men and women. Although it does not play very well anymore, as it has been strongly challenged by the increasing autonomy women have, and the decreasing self-confidence men have, this pattern still exists.

Girlfriends are the foundation of a balanced woman. Only a woman can fully understand the subtlety and complexity of female behavior. We all have different lives. However, we women all obey the same physiological rules that deeply connect us to each other and to the universe. It is critical that we reconnect regularly with this pure female being that we all share. Some may laugh thinking that women chattering to each other could achieve that. When the public persona leaves the scene, well, it does. Women's conversations have been undermined. They have been perceived as superficial because they rarely revolve around politics, careers, or sports, favorite male subjects. What is misunderstood is that women's conversations follow a spiral that begins large and narrows down to the point: rarely do women get straight to the point. They slowly put in place the setting to share what is important. They disclose their feelings until the solution to their problem sprouts in their head. Friends might suggest this or that; ultimately, though, each woman does what she truly feels is right. What has been suggested was not pointless however, because it helped the receiver of these suggestions feel appreciated and loved.

Few men understand this process or use it to communicate. Men have a radically different way of communicating and connecting with each other. The fact that women connect with each other less and less is detrimental to any relationship with a man, because the woman transfers her need to talk things through onto her male partner. He does not understand it, he is not equipped to deal with it, and he does not want to share his own problems. The misplacement leads to a buildup of frustrations on both sides.

Everything in life is about timing, but not everything is good all the time. Sharing with your partner is not good all the time either. We have been so obsessed with breaking the social barriers that the constant need to share has spread to all relationships, leading to detrimental confusion: parents are their kids' friends, men and women expect each other to be their buddy as well as their sex partner. Just like one size fits all, it fits no one really well. Shrinks of all kinds will never replace the bond two women can create. We all face many challenges; we all have very low moments when we wonder how we will cope with the next day. We all have less-than-perfect children that push our buttons regularly. It is okay. It is life. No one lives his or her life better than you do. Even those who have no children have other issues. Those who pretend differently are simply in denial. So we should share some time, some conversations, and be kind enough to listen to our trusted friends' concerns and happy moments. It will help them and it will help us. Even if all problems find first a solution within us, the road to the solution might be our friends' perspective.

Men, on the other hand, tend to shut down when they are stressed. Talking is the last thing they want to do; distraction and action for them are the two most powerful stress relievers. Television and the internet are the primary choice of distraction because they demand very little energy. Exercise and sex are the first choice of stress-relieving action: they both produce endorphins and boost the serotonin level. Most men, as a result, feel rather inadequate in handling their female partner's stress, and most women are close to being a nuisance when they think they are helping their male partner. And they blame him for shutting down. Men shut down mostly because expressing signs of weakness has been life-threatening for many centuries. Men are competitors and power seekers: they thrive in competitions of all kinds where the strongest, fastest, and smartest wins. There is no room for vulnerability in competitions. Although today, a lot of men use sport as a proxy for their competitive needs, the survival mechanism triggered remains deeply entrenched. Therefore the slightest stress triggers the fight or flight reaction, and talking is for tea time.

All over the world men are taught from an early age that they should not cry, that they should be tough, and that they should be strong. The ultimate power for men is that place where we are not vulnerable anymore, where we are in control. The propensity to abuse power is directly linked to the fear of being vulnerable. Obsessing over control is delusional. As men start to accept feeling vulnerable, their instinct to shut down will not be as strong. Will they talk more in stressful times? Maybe, but most importantly they will be more aware of the difficulty for their partner in coping with the stress they bring to the relationship. When we pause and reflect, we realize how little we control, and the amazing discovery that follows is that that lack of control is fine. The sooner we understand that the happier we are. If we wonder why women are more resilient and have a longer life expectancy than men, it is interesting to think that they have never been under any pressure to be tough and strong, and never cry. In fact the opposite is associated with femininity. This stereotypically feminine sensitivity is also perceived as weakness. All of the generations of women who have struggled to find a place in the business world would agree that there is no place for sensitivity there. It is starting to change though. More and more women dare to be who they are in their business environment, Oprah Winfrey being a famous example. Being vulnerable is not about being weak, it is acknowledging what we feel and respecting it. Shame usually stops men from acknowledging what they feel whenever the feeling is associated with weakness – whether it is weakness or not.

The direct consequence of men and women's differences in relieving stress is usually that men shut down precisely when women most need to talk. This is one of the highlights of John Gray's most recent book to date, Mars on Ice Venus on Fire[82], and it explains so many misunderstandings within a couple. Women process and solve issues while they talk about them; sharing is for them essential, especially when they are stressed. While doing so, they show their vulnerability, and their partner, challenged by this vulnerability, has one thing in

---

82 http://www.ezcouple.com/marsvenus

mind: solving the problem as soon as possible, hoping that it will quiet their wife. What they don't understand is that women never talk to get answers from others; they don't come to their partner with an issue for them to solve. No, what they want is a discussion that will help them find their own solution. Often as a result, these discussions are deeply frustrating for men... and for women. And stressful times do not help.

Men's acceptance of their own vulnerability will help them understand their partner's need to talk, but it will not make them choose conversation as an emotional release. To believe the contrary would be to misunderstand the true nature of the male mindset. They may need to talk at some point but not in the heat of the moment. Women are better off sharing whatever is worrying them with a reliable girlfriend than with their partner. While men release stress by relaxing through physical activity, talking is not a stress reliever for them; on the contrary, if they have some kind of emotional build-up, it generates stress. Two girlfriends sharing their feelings both benefit from that experience. We all go through struggles at one time or another. It is part of life. When a woman looks for a quick solution, she should go directly to her partner. Men are extraordinarily pragmatic short-term problem-solvers, leading straight to a rational solution. The solution a woman reaches after thinking and talking about the problem will be the right one for her. There is no one better than another woman to understand the meandering solving process of a female mindset. As the stress is lowered during the conversation she has, her perspective on the problem gradually changes as well, opening doors for new outcomes.

If men and women both understand and respect their own needs in order to relieve stress, they are more likely to avoid arguments caused by their own tension.

Part 3: Factors To Consider for Physical Intimacy In The Long Run

∽

We all know that physical intimacy is critical to any relationship. It is a non-verbal way to express love. It is also the deepest way to feel alive. When it comes to a couple, physical intimacy implies sexual intercourse.

We would gain a lot if we started to view physical intimacy as a whole, and sexual contact as only a part of that. Sex in a relationship has become a sensitive subject because the reference point is the first few years of any relationship, when passion, usually combined with hormonal needs, dictates the experience. Once again it is critical to understand the gender differences in depth in order to maintain some kind of sex life in the long run. One of the major problems long-term relationships have is a vanishing sex life. In addition to a lack of time, women and their relationship with their breasts are a leading cause. Let me tell you why. All women have a very complex relationship with their breasts. A vast majority is unhappy about them from a purely aesthetic perspective. What is less well-known is the suffering a woman endures because of these constantly changing glands. Two factors make breasts a sensitive subject for most, if not all, women:

Physical sensation

Psychological perception

Men primarily view female breasts as an enticing object for their sexual pleasure. Very often women meet them at this level, feeling great pleasure when this area of their body is gently and lovingly stimulated. What men tend to ignore, though, is that female breasts are a multifunctional organ primarily meant to feed a baby. While a baby sucking milk is definitely a major stimulation, it has nothing to do with the love games involving breast stimulation. I will only speak for myself, but let me tell you that I have never felt any arousal while breastfeeding any of my three kids. The mind then, is fully in mothering mode. So stimulation cannot be the only factor to place a woman in a sexual intercourse mode. The mind is what matters.

Depending on the mode she is in, whether it is sexy or mothering, a woman will be receptive or not to a sexual approach. No woman can easily switch from the mothering mode to the sexual mode, because once the mothering mode has kicked in, the sexual mode is ancillary. It is critical to understand this dual aspect of a woman's mind regarding her breasts because it is the only way for men to be appropriate and to feel successful in their sexual approach with their female partner.

In addition, many women are plagued with fibrocystic breasts. This condition can make any contact very painful. Most men are totally unaware of the discomfort it causes for a woman. This condition is extremely stressful for any woman because the medical community views fibrocystic breasts as potential breast cancer. As a result, routine X-rays, ultrasound, and MRIs are prescribed in the name of prevention because the worst is always expected. These examinations are not only invasive, they are also extensive, costly, and painful.

Simple measures successfully used long ago for women who had one or two nodules or cysts are never considered. Nobody tells women to make sure that their bra is properly sized and not blocking the very important lymphatic passageways to the armpit. The lymphatic system is critical to our immune system and yet, very few doctors think about it or suggest to their patient to have a professional lymphatic drainage done. Have a look at this diagram[83] that shows the lymph system in a woman, and you will understand why it is so important to have the breasts move freely on a regularly basis to let the lymph

83 http://www.ezcouple.com/diagrlymph

nodes drain well. Girls in puberty are advised to wear a bra as soon as their breasts start growing. The truth is that a healthy breast needs movement: blood and lymph circulation is accelerated with movement. Having girls wear a bra from an early age prevents them from becoming familiar with breasts' natural movement following the body's movement.

Bras are supposed to prevent sagging from a pure aesthetic perspective, masking what aging skin and weight will do naturally no matter what. It is far more important to teach girls with growing breasts to massage their breasts daily in order to prevent stagnation. A bra is only needed when sports practice makes breast movement uncomfortable. Unfortunately discouraging bras is unpopular because it is colored with a sense of being uncivilized. The staggering breast cancer rates found on breastcancer.org[84] should make us pause and reflect about what is the best interest for women. We are not going to stop wearing high heels because they ruin our backs. We are not going to stop wearing bras altogether because they might induce cancer growth. Are we? If we take our body to be the precious vehicle of our soul for a certain period, we might consider going beyond the high heels and the bras, and honor and respect that beautiful feminine body.

A successful sexuality starts with full acceptance of who we are beyond the male need for sexual intercourse. In unlocking the myths and fears around sex, The Good Girls' Guide To Great Sex[85], by Sheila Wray Gregoire, is an interesting book. I really like her Christian perspective and that she finds allusions to sex in the New and Old Testaments! I was raised as a Catholic, and flesh was only associated with sin, then. Her religious perspective on sex is refreshing. It is based on the idea that the married couple mirrors the relationship between God and the Church, with sex as the ultimate connection between the two. I am sure the Catholic priests who taught me catechism would choke reading this, which made reading it even more enjoyable. I have some reservations, however, about her deduction that the female body ultimately belongs to the man at a spiritual level during sex. Although she does not say so, this implies that the man would play the role of God and the woman would be the Church, who is supposed to surrender. Here is what she says:

"In sex, we're not just desiring each other: we're expressing something of God's relationship with us. And in this, we're playing roles: we Good Girls are the brides, the ones who are being wooed. Our husbands are the bridegrooms, the pursuers. That's why all of us women, in the height of sexual tension, will at times long just to be "devoured', to be "taken", and men often experience the urge to comply! For men, it's saying, "This is mine." For women, it's saying, "I'm not my own." It's actually a beautiful picture of how God longs to see us surrender. And it can only occur between a man and a woman. It can't work between two of the same sex, because the very illustration is meant to be between two very different beings: God and the church. There is no equality in sex. That does not mean that there's not spiritual equality in our relationship, or equality in household tasks or any of those other things we debate when it comes to gender roles. But in sex, there is just difference---and it's that difference that's sexy, exciting, attractive, and intoxicating." (p.164)

When I read that, the feminist in me starts screaming. No offense to men, but it is a big stretch to consider them even remotely at that level: Men, perfect god, and we women, sinful church who must surrender? Seriously? She thinks that difference is the basis of all good sex; and the next conclusion she draws is that same-sex couples can never reach sexually similar heights and spirituality because they are not different enough. This is overlooking the dynamic of homosexual couples that very often mimic heterosexual ones: I don't see why this differentiation would not play out in the bedroom as well. In addition, even if I understand her intention to be spiritual, I disagree with any statement that would place women as inferior under any circumstances. This is a very dangerous assumption in the light of all the abuse women have for centuries suffered from men whether inside or outside of a marriage. A woman's body never belongs to anybody but herself, even when she has another human being inside herself. It is unacceptable to think differently if we want women's expansion and growth for a truly balanced relationship with men.

You will note that I never talk about equality, which I believe is a faulty concept, utterly delusional. Equality may go well with rights, but it never suits individuals, especially when it comes to sex. The key word here is mutual rather than equal. A man and a woman, in a relationship that lasts, will have a fulfilling sexual life with one another if they make the necessary steps to understand and respect the other all day long. The bedroom needs to be a safe haven for both, with or without sex, depending on what happened during the day: there should be no agenda, schedule, or anything like that for sex. It all depends on you and your life partner, and what you both want. If you are not satisfied with your sex life, ask yourself what you are doing wrong. How is your communication with your partner? Are you sure nothing is missing in your interactions outside of sex? Sex offers us the opportunity to bring the relationship to a different level, but only if both partners feed that relationship on a daily basis. This is why I call sex the icing on the cake.

Part 4: Overcome The Challenge Of Eating Healthfully In Your Household

As much as I feel it is an absolute necessity to eat healthfully in order to stay in control of your mood while keeping any disease at bay, I know that it is impractical for most couples. The very first reason is that in most cases, it implies a drastic change of habits that will initially cause uncomfortable cravings and detoxification. In other words, you need to leave your comfort zone to incorporate new habits that will save you a great deal of time, stress, money, and may even save your life... in the long run. Well, if it is a shared decision, it is possible. But if only one partner has decided to change her or his diet, then that person will face major resistance at all family meals. And that would be an additional stress, unsustainable in the long run. Eating healthfully is a way to prevent further issues and stay in control of your mood.

Acting preventively has never been a huge success with human beings except when judicious marketing and big money are at stake. Vaccinations are a striking example. As is well stated in <u>Food Matters movies</u>[86], which I highly recommend that you watch, diseases not health make a lot of money. So eating healthfully is a personal decision with an initial cost that will make it very hard for any well-intentioned person to put in place if he or she is alone.

The second reason is that junk food is fast and easy. Raw food advocates will tell you that juicing is easy, but the truth is that nothing is easier than a fast-food drive-thru after work to get a full meal that will please the sleeping taste buds of the whole family. No grocery shopping, no meal preparation, no dishes, no convincing needed to feed the kids. How can you beat that? But eating this way is a vicious

---

86 http://www.ezcouple.com/fdmatters

cycle because the more you eat junk food, the less energy you have to cook proper food, and you never feel full, so you will most likely snack on an easy, super-salty or super-sweet snack before your next junk meal. Morgan Spurlock, in Super Size Me has bravely shown where this type of diet leads. And you could not be more wrong if you think that this is only the case if you eat only that type of fast food. Of course, less poison is better than more, but it nonetheless remains poison.

Health is a key factor for a thriving libido and a good energy level. So what can be done? Start by taking digestive enzymes to make sure you digest what you eat, and you have a regular bowel movement. Enzymes are not a free ticket to junk food; they just help your digestive system. If you combine them with probiotics you really give your digestive system a boost. Is that good enough? No, it is only a start. I don't think people make drastic changes spontaneously in one go. They need a trigger, whether a scare or a gradual process that makes the change possible. See your path to healthful eating as a ladder. It would be rather difficult to jump to step number ten when you start at zero, wouldn't it? It is the sure way to stay at the first level. It had better be a slow, gentle process, and you need your partner's participation.

The recalcitrant partner may be sensitive to the metaphor I will use now. Your body is the vehicle for your soul. Its health has a direct impact on your quality of life. Think of it as if it were your car. Most people treat their car extremely well, especially men. So what about treating your body just like you treat your car? Your car needs oil, so do you. You are a little more sophisticated than a car, so you need several oils, unrefined organic oils: coconut oil and olive oil, primarily. Your car needs water, and so do you, big time! Know that dehydration first affects the brain, and it is a simple cause of constipation. We usually forget to drink water when we are stressed, and it is precisely the time we should drink more in order to release the toxins created by the oxidation process. Your car needs a specific fuel, so do you! But first, as your body is not new, you need… an oil change! In terms of your body, this means cleansing or detoxification. There are two ways, one harder and one easier. Purists would say you need both. But just like with your car, you don't want to spend too much money, time, or energy on maintenance. So the easy way is colonics. I am not talking about the enema you get from the first pharmacy – that is as disgusting as it is impractical. There are now places you can go where it is a no-brainer process: you do the colonics yourself in a big bathtub, nobody sees your private parts, and within an hour, you have emptied your colon of all the waste and toxins, filled it with good bacterial flora (probiotics), and you are good to go with a new start. For more information, check the <u>Lighten Up Health Center</u>[87] in Orange County, California, to learn more about the process. It is a safe and clean place to try this procedure. If you have a relaxing lymph drainage session before the colonic, you will accelerate the detoxification process and make it pain free. The harder way to detoxify is with herbs and juice fasting, and you still need to make sure your colon gets rid of its junk throughout the process. For a family, this type of detoxification is impractical: your children will eat normally, and the temptation to give up will be too strong.

Following the car analogy, you must upgrade to premium fuel and you must move.

---

87 http://www.ezcouple.com/lghtctr

Upgrade to premium fuel

That means eat organic and:

• Add green leafy vegetables.

• Add colorful salads with olive oil and lemon dressing that you make.

• Add walnuts, almonds, cashew nuts, hazelnuts, and seeds (sunflower, pumpkin, sesame, linseed, etc.).

• Add vitamin C, omega-3, probiotics, and a good multivitamin.

• Replace sugar with xylitol, or stevia if you can cope with the taste.

• Eat organic, grass-fed meat.

• Drink at least five glasses of plain water a day. Add a drop of lemon essential oil to make it more flavorful if the idea of plain water is too unappetizing. No, it won't damage your enamel, because lemon, when metabolized by the body, becomes alkaline-forming.

• Add coconut oil to your diet. It is the best cooking oil you can possibly use. The benefits of coconut oil are countless: ketones found in coconut oil may treat and reverse Alzheimer's disease by providing an alternative fuel for brain cells and protecting them.

Check out Dr. Mary Newport's blog[88] for the latest findings on ketones and neuro-degenerative brain diseases. You can also take a look on YouTube[89] at her own experience with coconut oil and her husband's diagnosis with Alzheimer's disease. The latest research findings can also be found in this article on the "Neurobiology of Aging"[90] published in autumn 2012. The ketogenic diet based on ketone ingestion with complete suppression of carbohydrates shows documented results with epilepsy, and also seems to starve cancer

88 http://www.ezcouple.com/keton
89 http://www.ezcouple.com/vid10
90 http://www.ezcouple.com/antiaging

cells. So it is a good idea to substitute coconut oil for all your cooking oils, and eat at least two tablespoonfuls a day. You can find information on my blog post[91] about how we use coconut oil in our family; you will be amazed.

For examples and guidance on how to eat healthfully, I really like the Green Smoothie Girl[92], Robyn Openshaw's web site. Not only is she didactic, she is also realistic. You can check her website and this video in particular[93], in which she explains how to choose your green vegetables. She provides valuable information that can be helpful for any health-conscious person. She also offers a book called "8 Week Menu Planner"[94] that paves the way to healthful eating: you have three meals a day, menus and a supply list for eight weeks really worth investigating. They passed her children's test!

If you give your body the proper fuel, it will run longer. More importantly, it will give you the energy you need to accomplish what your mind decides to do. If you still think eating healthfully is no fun, spend some time with a relative who is struggling with a chronic disease, severe or not, and tell me how fun that is. When cancer is on the rise, when cardiovascular disease is common, when asthma is on the rise, as well as ADD and ADHD, I believe you want to do for yourself and your loved ones what it takes to be and stay healthy. I truly wish that Steve Jobs' death at 56 serves as a wakeup call. If this extraordinary man could not be saved with all the means he had to get the best doctors in the world, what are our chances? So don't wait until you are there to make the necessary changes.

---

91 http://www.ezcouple.com/blogcoconut
92 http://www.ezcouple.com/gsg
93 http://www.ezcouple.com/vidgsgs
94 http://www.ezcouple.com/foodplan

Move your body

Swimming, walking fast, and among indoor exercise (although nothing forbids that you do it in the privacy of your back yard!), sexual intercourse, are the top exercises that will keep every cell of your body in shape.

Similar to your car, if you don't use your body, meaning if you don't use the approximately 640 skeletal muscles that need your will to get moving, on a regular basis, you are heading for problems very similar to those you would have with your car.

So please, move! And move with your partner. That should be fun!

Last but not least, get the proper tools to make your life easy when you decide to cook. I love the Thermomix TM31 from Vorverk, a German appliance that is so easy to use and easy to clean that once you know how to operate it, making your own juice, your own soups, or your own meals will be a no-brainer. You can go to my blog[95] for more information about this amazing appliance. Getting the right kitchen tools is sometimes the key to making the right changes. Be curious about what you eat; check common beliefs, check how you feel when you eat this or that. This is the best way to find the diet that will suit you. What we know for a fact is that the Standard American Diet (SAD)[96] leads to diseases. When you start eating healthfully you discover new flavors and new textures. Make it a family adventure. It is a hit or miss process, but soon you will have recipes that you all love. You will do a great service to yourself, your relationship, and your family.

---

95 http://www.ezcouple.com/tm31
96 http://www.ezcouple.com/cdc4

8

THE FUTURE OF RELATIONSHIPS
IN PIONEERING TIMES

We are the first generations to have so many opportunities. The scope of choice is such that discernment is necessary in every area of our lives. Our brains will probably adjust to the massive input they are exposed to every day. For now though, we must take measures to make sure we don't drown in the sea of solicitations.

Part 1: Managing An Overwhelming Schedule
∽

You read and hear everywhere that we should practice mindfulness and meditation in order to stay healthy and enjoy life. The reality, though, is that days are so packed that there is no room for anything that is not compulsory. Yet research proves that health significantly depends on how we deal with stress. The fact that we're all stone-aged minds in a technological 21st century not surprisingly triggers stress. The vast possibilities offered by the internet, the amazing knowledge available to anyone with a connection, makes the world both fascinating and exhausting. When you add to that the cumulatively maddening schedules of your children, what is left? We must all learn self-discipline when it comes to screen time. It is so easy to be browsing all day!

We need one day off per week. Our body and our mind need that day off.

EVERYBODY complains about the pace of life being too fast but nobody does anything about it. Except for entrepreneurs, nobody works seven days a week. Even entrepreneurs should have the self-discipline to squeeze one day off a week out of their calendar if they don't want to lose several years of their life as a result.

My beloved husband has well understood the concept; instead of one day, however, he has divided his day off so it is equally spread over two days. As a result, he does not have any day off per se.

Let's focus on that "per se" one second. The whole concept of a day off here in California is interesting: it is the day one does not go to work or school. The funny thing is that weekends are so filled with activities that they are busier than weekdays. This is not particular to California, though: it is a general trend in the western world where parents' anxiety meets with children's dictatorship. Those with children are running from event to game in the belief that the more the better. And those without kids feel compelled to do something active, outside of their home… something fun… hopefully.

I might be giving into the preconceived ideas Americans already have about the French, but I will take the risk: a day off, guys, is a day…OFF. It is OFF anything that is not you and your inner circle. And a day is 24 hours.

How many millions of dollars are spent on anti-aging this or that? Watch this interesting Ted Talk video where <u>Dan Buettner</u>[97] explains his findings on longevity. You will be amazed by what you hear. Longevity depends on lifestyle, diet, and, last but not least, connections. If you believe the studies mentioned in that Ted Talk, sticking to the lifestyle of a twenty-year-old no matter what will make us die sooner rather than later. I don't suggest yet that we all go to church on Sunday, or synagogue on Saturday, according to whatever is closer to one's home and beliefs, to help fight off the social pressure that distracts us from our day off. But we can't expect to sustain the unsustainable for very long. In the U.S., it seems that people spend their life on a treadmill that never stops. Why is it so difficult to apply to us what seems logical for any electronic or mechanic appliance we have? Even your computer gets turned off regularly, and if it does not, you endure painful minutes of updates to have it run smoothly again. We all know that, don't we?

We, human beings, are cyclical: our energy is not linear. And if we are not totally disconnected from ourselves, we feel the need to slow down. Life is so demanding though, that the first signs of fatigue are very often overlooked, and we get used to living with an average energy level that gradually decreases. A few months ago I went to see my beloved doctor for a checkup: when I told her I was tired, she told me again to slow down. And I heard myself saying once more: "Yes, but…" It is this "yes, but" that kills us slowly but surely. Off the top of my head, I can give you at least ten reasons why I can't have a proper day off during which I'd do nothing, except feed myself and my family. The problem, though, is that a busy seven-day week is

---

97 http://www.ezcouple.com/vid11

not sustainable in the long run. What is the connection with my goal to help couples thrive, you may wonder? Well, don't you think that when you're stretched, therefore stressed, your way of handling your relationship is affected? Health is taken for granted until something goes wrong. You now understand how critical it is for your relationship to be healthy, don't you? A day off fosters health. Big time! It allows you to slow down, to unwind and, most importantly to reflect.

Life is too short to let it go by without making sure we are where we are supposed to be. Otherwise, when can we ask ourselves these critical questions?

> Am I happy?
>
> Am I comfortable with my life as it is today?
>
> What can I improve?
>
> Who would I like to spend more time with?

Asking these questions can be scary, but how can we improve anything in our life without asking them? Quieting the mind fosters creativity and it allows us to reflect and ask these difficult questions. Prayer is nothing but reflection silencing the mind. It does not have to be religious, but it certainly is spiritual. And whether we like it or not, we are spiritual beings. Ignoring that part of ourselves does not lead to inner peace. Reflection offers the possibility of reconnecting with who we are regardless of external pressures; it then allows us to give and receive from a neutral place.

Let me explain.

Too often relationships are reduced to an exchange of expectations more or less met. The key to a thriving long-term relationship is to feel good first. Most people wait for their partner to do this or that or stop doing this or that in order to feel at ease. They therefore hand over their happiness to their partner, instead of taking responsibility for it. Nobody else knows where our happiness lies. Nobody else can guide us to do the things that will make us happy. What feels right is an inside job. Is there anything more personal than feeling? How do we expect to know what we feel if we don't quiet our mind?

Until I was convinced that a day off was a necessity, I was amazed that whenever my husband and I would go away together, we would not talk much for a few days. These days we were each recuperating, and no energy was available for the other. Our energy tank was so empty that we could only cope with ourselves. Then we would rediscover the other without any agenda, without any pressure. For most long-term couples, especially when children are in the picture, there are so many things to deal with on a daily basis that communication is similar to that you would have with a business partner. That does not foster romance, or boost any woman's libido.

Remember what it was like at the beginning of the relationship. Your relationship came first; you never let your daily lives spoil the chemistry. Well, if you make it compulsory, a day off can bring that back. The day will unfold, and soon you will be surprised by the difference in your home atmosphere. One day with no outings, no driving, no shopping, no phone, no email, and no TV. Your children will be calmer, and your bedtime will be nicer. Don't expect an enthusiastic response from your family at first, and it may be difficult to put it in place. By the way, this is where religion can become handy! All religions advocate a day off once a week for prayers and rest. If you stick to it, soon everybody will love it without really understanding why. Soon you will only do what truly means to you on that day. That evening, that night, you will not go to bed exhausted, and you will have a sense of control over your life that you may not have in your daily routine.

If we collectively decided to stop the madness, of course it would make things much easier. Once again we can't wait for a majority to act before we act for ourselves. Scientific findings on the benefits of meditation are slowly reaching the mainstream. There are more and more studies showing how stress shortens the telomere – a piece of DNA attached like a tail to each cell. Once the telomere is too short the cell simply dies. This is what we call aging. In 2009 <u>Dr. Doris Taylor spoke with Krista Tippett</u>[98] (interview already mentioned at the beginning of this book) about stem cells and mentioned a study done on Matthieu Ricard, the French Buddhist monk, before and after he meditates. The study found that his stem cells had increased in number by 40% after 15 minutes of meditation. Our brain and body need breaks. And if we want the idea of family to be appealing to future generations we had better change how we spend our time, fast.

We will soon realize that we all, more or less consciously, feel the heavy pressure on our shoulders. As a result we follow a rhythm that controls us, and happiness is not on the menu. If you miss a birthday party, a sports game, or any other event just to make some space in your life, it won't be the end of the world. It might just be the beginning of your world. It might give you the opportunity to change your perspective. Worrying about what others think is bound to lead nowhere, because you will never know what they truly think. What matters is what you think, what feels good for you. We should all rebel from the dictatorship of sports, over-scheduling millions of kids in the hopes of finding the next Tiger Woods, Kobe Bryant, or you-name-it sports star.

Soccer used to be the sport for everyone: all you need is a ball or something that looks like a ball. In many countries kids play soccer with whatever they can find that rolls. Some of the best players in the world come from these countries. Soccer opened the doors for a

---

98 http://www.ezcouple.com/nprob

better life for kids from poor countries. Now there is so much money at stake that professionalism is expected from ten-year-olds, even if a good 90% of these children have no future in soccer. Why can't we just play for fun? Why are the commitments for any one sport so demanding that they forbid playing others? If our children can't try different things between the ages of nine and twenty, when will they be able to? After school activities have become so serious that they are worse than school. Our kids need to dream, and so do we. Time management should be reviewed in all households. The more we slow down one complete day a week, the less difficult that will be. All it takes is determination and courage.

Part 2: Ethics And Values Are What We Need Most

We need respect to be at the forefront of our behavior. The way we behave all comes down to values, ethics, and a clear understanding between the right and the wrong. The line between the two may be really fine at times, but nevertheless there is a line. We should all make sure we are on the right side of this border. Values are not innate. They are learned over the years until they become second nature. It takes a daily check nowadays to make sure we stick to what we believe in. Most of today's problems stem from a lack of values. Many leaders do not seem to have this internal compass that guides them to do the right thing, especially if it goes against popular beliefs or it delays gratification. Doing what is right is never easy: in fact, in this economic world, it goes against the never-ending quest for easy profits. At the end of the day, though, we are nothing, and we don't belong to ourselves but to something greater than we are. Silencing the ego should therefore be the priority. Personal pride is a natural reward of any good action, but it should not blind us. The deep roots of the economic crisis in which all western nations seem to have sunk stem from greediness, corruption, and lies. In order to avoid this, for EZcouple.com, I made decisions about the functionalities of the site that may not serve my immediate best interest from a business perspective. EZcouple will take care of your personal relationship, the most intimate one; it did not make sense to me to make any of the personal data of EZcouple members' area public, for everyone to see. It will be a membership site just like other social networks, but the comparison stops there. Unlike other "social" networks I refuse to trick the user and falsely increase the number of people who could join my site. For instance, EZcouple will never ask you if you want the site to invite your contacts on your email, or regularly send invitations on your behalf to your contacts until you realize that you must disable that feature in your account settings. You, the user, decide to enter the email address of the friend or the relative you want to join your account to help you: one and only one invitation email is sent at that point. That's it. EZcouple's users will not be subscribed to my newsletter by default. Communication with the user is limited to the strictly necessary. I want to build trust more than anything else. I believe that EZcouple will work for the greater good. I think that there is an urgent need for it, to save many couples from the boredom of traditional interaction that has become more annoying than anything else after many years together. I also want it to be a tool, a tool that will help men understand the simple things and actions their wives truly need and want.

The usual cleavage between men and women should be history. With the many challenges we have to face as a community, as humankind, it is urgent that we bring peace home so we don't waste our energy in private arguments that consume us. We would not have made so much progress since the beginning of civilization if we all had the same skills, if we all thought the same way. Diversity is at the source of various creations. It is an unbelievable asset to be able to share our lives with someone of the opposite gender. It reminds us to be humble, open, and ready to learn. It mitigates human propensity to ignore and fear that which is different. The bonding between a man and a woman is a source of creation on many levels: both genders' mindsets and perspectives are required to meet the challenges that we face.

Throughout history, what is new has often been unsettling at first, yet I do not think that the scope of changes and challenges has ever been as great as it is now. Technology changes it all for everyone. Never before were we able to spread a piece of news as quickly or as far as we can today. Never before could world events affect our lives like a tsunami wherever we live, whatever we do. Never before have families been challenged the way they are today. Never before, has a virtual world with real people behind it run our lives. Technology is the greatest thing that has happened to humanity in a long time. It allows connections over distances that were inconceivable twenty years ago. Each week when I meet virtually with my team, I feel blessed to belong to these fascinating times. We all manage to talk and work together while being on two different continents and in three time zones. We have never physically met, yet we succeed in communicating and working efficiently. The potential for improvement in our lives brought by the internet is just emerging. Yet, as you know from the comic book Spiderman, with great power comes great responsibility. The internet is, to some extent, like the wild west: it is a new land where the laws that elsewhere apply to everyone do not seem to apply. Privacy is elusive, and ownership of one's data is uncertain. And worse, kids are thrown into a trend of disclosing what should remain private without even being able to understand the scope of what they are doing. We have news of kids committing suicide because the scope of exposure of any data on the internet can be exponential. A prank that would have had limited consequences before the internet can now have an unbearable social impact. The key again is ethics. Ethics are the moral compass that determines how we treat others. If we use ethics to guide us in every decision we make, we are less likely to make harmful decisions. Ethics reveal the true will to be a better person not only for ourselves but also for the others. I hope EZcouple will be successful. Of course I will be proud of myself if it is, but ultimately I want it to serve others, to be a useful addition to their lives. I would love it if it helped couples to connect or reconnect on a deeper level so they enjoy their relationship. Divorces are a plague that costs not only to the couple and their children, but also to the community as a whole dearly. More than ever, children need the support of both parents; they need their guidance. How do you teach respect, the values of commitment and perseverance when you are unable to have a respectful and loving relationship with your spouse, whom, at one point, you chose? Facts are what matter. Children don't care about what one says, they care and watch what we do. They forge their own idea of the world based on their experience. I really want my kids to understand that what matters in life is having a purpose, a goal that will do some good. I want them to know that they don't belong to themselves but to something much greater than themselves. Finally I want them to understand that only love, true love is fulfilling. Only love leads to happiness. Money and power don't. They are only tools that can serve equally the good or the bad. I am blessed with smart children. I hope they will make good use of this intelligence. Moral values remind us that our actions have consequences that affect others, that we are all interconnected, and that it is in our best interest to care for the others because they will most likely care for us in return. When you think about manners, why are they so important? Manners make human interactions pleasant, regardless of how we each feel. They serve the ultimate belief that the other deserves to be cared for. They are the reminder that our tendency to be selfish and self-centered is unsustainable at a community level. Finally, manners serve values I've been advocating. And these values fight against our propensity to be greedy, careless, and unethical. No human being is born with values. We all learn them. It is not an easy task for parents, but it is part of our job. Once again kids learn mostly by watching their parents. Walking away at the first sign of difficulty demonstrates a lack of commitment. I wrote in length about the ripple effects of divorce. The notion of respect I keep referring to, depends on the core values in our interaction with others; it is not the compliance with a belief system most likely outdated. Doing what is right is not necessarily the easy road, but it is the most fulfilling one.

Part 3: Freedom Is Not A Wilderness

We all have more freedom than ever before, and limitations have in most cases been internalized. What Seth Godin, the entrepreneur and author I mentioned in chapter 5, calls the lizard brain, the amygdala, operates to keep us "safe" from experiencing new things. Personal work is therefore essential in order to achieve more, or better. My personal motto has always been "quality over quantity." Very often this position is not popular. It is perceived as elitist. The tribe concept, that is, groups, even very small ones, whose members are connected to each other by a common interest, as explained by Seth Godin (see chapter 5) will not suit everyone. Many people don't have a specific interest that will make them part of a tribe, or start a new one. Many still look for a guide, a general guide to follow, and that guide is defined by his or her popularity rather than by the value of his or her actions and ideas. Sudden national fame can make someone a guide for many people. Not everyone chooses to be discerning, and many will choose to rely on someone else's opinion instead. Fair enough. But if we want our personal relationship to last in this context of ultimate freedom, we must put in some effort. We must understand that the easy road is the one that has us giving up on our relationship at the very first big challenge. Any couple who has lasted many years knows that any relationship will face numerous obstacles. Every challenge in life is an opportunity to learn and grow. Overcoming difficulties in the relationship that you wanted to last in the first place means reaching aspects of yourself that you would otherwise have never suspected exist. To achieve balance, it helps to understand the interaction of the feminine and the masculine within ourselves. Anyone can now break off the relationship or divorce at the first sign of a challenge. Freedom mostly means that we have a choice. We can choose to grow or not. We can choose victimization or not. We can choose to stay trapped, overwhelmed, respected, or not. The work place is also changing by the day. The road to success is no longer as clear as it once was.

During these times of transition, a solid relationship to rely on is needed more than ever. Although marriage seems to be in decline, it remains the emotional base that gives us the strength to go beyond our fears and face the world to achieve more. It gives meaning to our lives beyond materialistic achievements. We live in a world of over-stimulation, of connections more meaningless than meaningful. Finding fulfillment is increasingly difficult because we are constantly overwhelmed by a multitude of choices. One would think that having more choices is a better option. This is true only if we have a strong sense of who we are and what we need. Being in a relationship helps us define what truly matters to us. The unexpected freedom we all have today gives us the possibility of initiating the change we want to see. More importantly we have a deeper understanding of the impact we have on one another. We can't control what our partner feels or thinks, but we influence our partner through what we think, feel, and believe. If we, as individuals, get closer to what is truly important, our life partner might or might not follow us on the same path.

Even if we have no clue what change it will bring, our internal work will initiate one. The outcome may not seem appealing at first, yet it is the only way to real discernment. Our western world is all about connections, about "friends", and yet, we all feel isolated like never before. I can't help but make the analogy to food in developed countries. Food is abundant and, yet, so little of it is nourishing. Again discernment is the only way to feed our body properly. Knowledge is everywhere, available for free as long as you have an internet connection. Once you start investigating food and nutrition, you will be amazed by how far from the truth you have been led. You will notice that your body's best interest is rarely taken into account. Similarly, one can have thousands of Facebook friends and at the same time no real friends. I encourage you to read this excellent article from the Boston Globe, "What does 'friend' mean now?"[99], by Joseph P Khan,, about the concept of "friend" and the impact of technology on it. In France we have a much more conservative approach towards the literal translation of "friend". We use "acquaintance" or the equivalent, to describe the person we know whenever the personal connection is not deep.

To me, a true friend implies an emotional connection with personal implications: here again comes vulnerability. With a true friend, we

99 http://www.ezcouple.com/bg0511

shed the public persona of who we would like to be for who we truly are, and we take the risk of being loved or rejected as we are. It takes a lot of time and effort to sustain and manage a true friendship, because we leave the surface to go deep into our lives. Our ego might feel good about a nice compliment on Facebook; our true self is still desperately looking for true love. The myth of the "friend" comes from the fact that social websites, in most cases, are a public arena. Unconditional love is not public: it is not light and superficial. It feeds on an interaction of feelings at a physical level, like all types of true love. My website EZcouple will be in total contrast to the trends on social networks. I have come to dislike the word "social" for the fuzzy concept it has become. EZcouple will not suit everyone; it is for the man and the woman in a relationship who love each other, and for those who love that couple enough to help them without public reward and congratulations. It is not socializing; it is giving in the pure sense of the term. It may make no marketing sense to conceive a project like mine. I feel, however, that we all thrive on authenticity. In relationships this is particularly important. The friends on EZcouple are the true friends, the ones with whom we have an emotional, personal and physical connection. The physical connection with your partner may be lacking at times, but initially this connection was really strong. The importance of this physical connection is worth emphasizing. Online social connections may be fulfilling to an extent, when we interact about similar interests, but they feed the mind more than they feed the heart. When you experience meeting in person for the first time someone with whom you have only communicated online, it feels awkward. The relationship has to become grounded on the physical plane: it has to start anew because it needs to incorporate the physical factor.

Online connections can stay virtual until you want them to reach the next level of intimacy, touching the heart. Real physical connection then becomes necessary. There is so much more to one being than one's mind and voice. All of our senses are stimulated when we actually meet someone: we feel that person. An energy imprint is memorized at an emotional level, and it resonates with us or not. The ultimate relationship outside the family and generational connections is the couple, the foundation of a new family. A long-term relationship is our very first opportunity for authenticity. It is the safe environment in which we can practice using our inner compass and learn to respect it. More than ever our inner compass or intuition is critical: discernment requires knowledge, but in the sea of information we have access to in any subject, knowledge requires discernment. Devoting time to something and having experience with it definitely help in distinguishing real knowledge from false. Nothing, however, is more efficient than the non-scalable, instant gut feeling one sometimes has. Freedom is not a wilderness if we respect and nurture what truly matters, whatever it is. The choice is ours.

CONCLUSION

Questioning and noticing are the two actions that make a difference today. We come from different cultures, different backgrounds, different locations, yet we all have in common the fact that we thrive on love. The very nature of the feeling is identical wherever we live. What is not is our ability to show our love. Culture is then the determining factor. Culture is similar to history; they are both valuable as long as we can put them in perspective.

What I have absolutely loved about my life for the past eleven years is that my beliefs have constantly been challenged. I have had the opportunity to realize how limiting it is for the mind to stay in its comfort zone. Many people never move far away from their hometown, and many people never feel this disconnection from what is known and familiar. Yet depths of knowledge result from that disconnection. Those who have lived in other countries know how disturbing the first few months in the new place can be; the discomfort is total because nothing is familiar. Questioning and noticing are then essential to survive. The word may sound strong, however the psychological shift one needs to go through to adjust to new terms is a form of survival. The life before is gone, and the new life is unfamiliar. We "forget" consciously or unconsciously what was difficult or less appealing and focus on what we liked and what we miss. So the mind embellishes the past until the present becomes bearable.

No matter how painful that process can be, it is an amazing learning experience that exemplifies what modern life is becoming. When your life is spent across the world from home, you look for connections with people based on what you value, what matters to you. Connections are no longer based on location or culture; they can form anywhere, and it takes time and energy to nurture them. All relationships are now following this tendency, even at an intimate level. Marriages can be dissolved almost overnight, and grown-up children might never contact their parents again if they don't wish to. Religion is vainly resisting this wave, and social pressure against it is almost nonexistent because communities are diffuse. Communities are now based on the similarities of heart and mind, regardless of location.

The good news is that relationships can now be truly meaningful: a lasting couple today can be proud; each partner has gone beyond his or her little ego to reach out to the other in such a way that the other feels compelled to stay. The dynamic of the relationship has been understood and valued. That success takes work, though, conscious and intentional work. Remember that exercising is a relatively new concept, resulting from our sedentary lives. To live well, we had to adapt and consciously decide that we would exercise to stay healthy; similarly we can no longer presume that our relationship will last without our conscious intervention to make it work. We must adapt: EZcouple.com is the very first site to help us do so.

My husband is my closest connection on every level. He is the only one besides me who truly knows who I am. His impact in my life is invaluable, and I believe the feeling is mutual. The strength we both have to face all the changes presented to us over the years is an extraordinary fuel that nourishes the heart, the mind, and the soul. We both know that the other is that loving shoulder we can rest on. After eighteen years together, my husband is my lover, my best friend, my coach, and my compass. He is the one with whom I always share what is most important to me. I deeply believe that I am a better person because of him. I wish that you, dear reader, can grow and find a better you with the help of your life partner. I hope this book guides you on the path of a fulfilling relationship. You might not agree with everything you have read. It does not matter. What matters is that you start questioning and noticing what is in your life.

With love,

Anne

ABOUT THE AUTHOR

As we encounter the first challenges in a relationship, we all look for advices that will help us solve our current problem in the long run. The drilling question about the best relationship advice we can get is rarely answered because each relationship has its own dynamic. Yet nothing beats experience. I have been in my relationship long enough to give you valuable insights. I am not you and you are not me, but I am sure that you will change your perspective on your own relationship after reading this book. We all know that a long-term relationship has rocky moments in the course of its life.

I have come to understand that there are key factors that one should closely watch in order to sail through the difficult times any relationship has in store. This book aims to raise your awareness about your own relationship.

Whether you want to save your marriage or simply improve your relationship, my experience will help you: I have walked the talk.

I am a French woman in my forties, married to a French man whom I deeply love. My husband and I have three multicultural children, and we all live in Southern California in the U.S. I am also the founder of EZcouple.com, previously PeaceReminder.com, a project I have been dedicated to, for close to five years.

When couples around me started to separate five years ago about ten or more years into their relationship, I thought that something should be done. Of course my own relationship was my first point of reference. At that time, I had been married for ten years, and before that my husband had been my boyfriend for four years. We were doing pretty well, still very much in love with each other. I then looked at my friends who were separating and I also listened to those who were unhappy in their relationships. I quickly found common ground in complaints of most women and while men's complaints had their own common ground. My focus was then to find out what had gone amiss and what could be done to prevent the collapse of a relationship meant to last.

I discovered that miscommunication and lack of efficient nurturing were at the root of the frustration for both men and women that preceded the collapse of the relationship.

I know all too well from my own experience as a child of divorce and as a lawyer that separations are very costly both financially and emotionally.

My goal is therefore to work on preventing such separations. I believe that long-term relationships are critical to a stable and harmonious society. I even believe that being in a long-term relationship makes us better people.

What qualifies me to offer you this kind of advice? In 2013 my husband and I celebrated our 15th anniversary; we have been together a total of nineteen years, and we both feel that we love each other even more than we did at the beginning of our relationship. We have three beautiful children, one teenage boy, one tween girl, and one seven-year-old boy. I am therefore quite aware of the challenges family life presents to any couple.

Besides, I have a unique international perspective, having lived and raised my children in France, Singapore, Hong Kong, and now in California. This experience is particularly useful in putting any social pressure in perspective.

I am primarily a certified lawyer by training, but I am also a passionate learner. When I feel the need to understand a field more, I learn as much as I can on any subject I find relevant. It is with this mindset that five years ago my interest on relationships, couples' therapies, and techniques to help solve relationship issues grew to become an area of expertise for me.

My personal experience, combined with my continually increasing knowledge, gives me a very pragmatic approach to improving relationships. I want results. I want to offer solutions that work without you having to revamp your whole life, or you and your spouse spending hours and money on a coach – or worse, with a divorce lawyer.

The task of saving your relationship from a detrimental boredom may seem huge when you see the divorce statistics numbers, but I believe that all it takes to go beyond our immediate selfish interest and search for long-term solutions is some common sense combined with the intention to make the relationship work.

Through this book, I share with you everything I know that can improve your life.

My goal is to improve our lives. To learn more about me and what I do, or to get in touch with me, please visit my blog at EZcouple.com.

www.ingramcontent.com/pod-product-compliance
Lightning Source LLC
Chambersburg PA
CBHW072135270326
41931CB00010B/1765